WORKING
WHILE BLACK

WORKING
WHILE BLACK

THE BLACK PERSON'S GUIDE
TO SUCCESS
IN THE WHITE WORKPLACE

SECOND EDITION

MICHELLE T. JOHNSON

FOREWORD BY JULIANNE MALVEAUX

Lawrence Hill Books

Library of Congress Cataloging-in-Publication Data
Johnson, Michelle T.
Working while black : the black person's guide to success in the white
workplace / Michelle T. Johnson. — 2nd ed.
    p. cm.
Includes bibliographical references and index.
ISBN 978-1-56976-346-9 (pbk.)
  1. African Americans—Employment—Psychological aspects. 2. Success
in business. I. Title.
HD8081.A65J64 2010
650.1089'96073—dc22

                                                    2010027728

Cover and interior design: Monica Baziuk
Cover photo: PBNJ Productions/Blend Images/Getty Images
Typesetting: Jonathan Hahn

Published by Lawrence Hill Books
An imprint of Chicago Review Press, Incorporated
814 North Franklin Street
Chicago, Illinois 60610
ISBN 978-1-56976-346-9
Printed in the United States of America
5   4   3   2   1

■

This book is dedicated to all the ancestors who made the opportunities possible, and to the descendants who endure and made the book necessary to write.

■

CONTENTS

■

ACKNOWLEDGMENTS

■

WITH THE SECOND EDITION of this book comes another group of supporters who helped make my writing and serving happen. So along with my stalwart supporters Ethel, Cliffie, Adrienne, and many others, I would particularly like to thank Ora Stafford, Jahi Boseda, and Joy Springfield.

DISCLAIMER

■

Every incident, person, and example in this book is either a true story or based on a true story. Because of the nature of my job as a mediator and former employment attorney in a law firm (and because I have friends and associates who will hunt me down), names are not used and, when necessary, identifying details are changed to protect privacy.

This is not, I repeat, *not* legal advice. Please do not let any comments in this book serve as your sole or motivating basis for doing or saying anything that will have legal ramifications. If you really think you've got a problem, talk to a friend, a counselor, a spiritual adviser, or an attorney and get advice from a professional who knows the specific facts of your situation. Refer to the resources in the back of this book for further assistance and inspiration.

FOREWORD

Julianne Malveaux

"Without work all life is rotten," wrote the French novelist and essayist Albert Camus. "But when work is soulless, life stifles and dies." I cannot read the Camus quote without thinking of the centrality of work in our lives and the many ways work has evolved from simply a means for survival and sustenance into something that infuses significant meaning in our lives. To be sure, most Americans must work in order to survive—despite the unequal distribution of wealth, only a small percentage of us are "trust fund babies." For many of us, the workplace is the place where we spend a third of our lives, form relationships, develop social networks, search for meaning, and make a contribution to the world. Work doesn't always work. Men and women struggle with balancing work and family, many chafe under unsafe and unfair working conditions, others come face to face with discrimination in the workplace, and millions strain to find work because they both want and need it.

The workplace, then, is a complex place for most of those who inhabit it in good times and all the more challenging during this Great Recession, when the threat of layoffs and reorganization adds nuance to existing challenges. Furthermore, the workplace has been transforming for the past several decades. Instead of holding career jobs, today's average learner will have fourteen jobs by age thirty-eight, or a new job every year and a half. Globalization, the proliferation of technology, and demographic shifts have made the workplace far more competitive. And people continue to work because they must, both for survival and meaning.

What happens when you add race to the contemporary workplace? Michelle Johnson offers sociopolitical observations, advice, helpful workplace tips, and old-fashioned mother wit in this absorbing book. Being black is a full-time job, she observes, and you don't even get paid for it. While you won't get paid, you will pay, she says, and then delineates the many ways that African American workers pay the "black tax" on the job. Johnson acknowledges that the workplace is challenging for everyone, and 85 percent of the African American work experience is similar to that of others. The rub is the remaining 15 percent, those differences that are often unspoken and unacknowledged but painfully real for those who experience them. In unpacking the 15 percent, Johnson has produced a must-read for African American job seekers, those facing employment challenges, and those seeking to understand their own work styles. She divides black workers into survivors, strivers, thrivers, and drivers and contrasts the ways these folks might deal with race matters in the workplace. This useful division of work motivations makes this book also helpful for those who, regardless of race, want to understand the actions and reactions of their fellow workers and employees.

Why is a book like this needed in a so-called post-racial era? The answer, of course, is that we are not post-racial yet. In the employment arena, during this Great Recession, this is confirmed by data that shows, for example, that in June 2010 the unemployment rate for whites was 8.6 percent but nearly twice as high, 15.6 percent, for African Americans. It is confirmed by academic studies that show that Tammy is more likely to get a job than Tamika. The mean income among African Americans is still just 60 percent of white median income, and even when African Americans and whites have identical educations and work experience, there is an income gap.

The hard data suggest that the work experience for African Americans and whites is different, and subjective perceptions of the national climate underscore the suggestion. Consider the Shirley Sherrod case, in which an African American employee of the Department of Agriculture was unjustly accused of racism after a rogue Tea Party activist released a badly edited tape that seemed to show her making a loaded racial statement. In less than seventy-two hours she was fired, offered her job back, and given a presidential apology. The incendiary nature of the race debate is such that smug whites used her out-of-context comments as an example of reverse racism, while some hasty African Americans, eager to please, condemned Sherrod as quickly as whites did without bothering to hear the whole story. This story dominated the airwaves for nearly a week. What was the watercooler conversation around it? While the Sherrod situation may have had little to do with the work that any individual does, the heat around it must have seeped into some workplaces. Are there risks and rewards for black and white workers in engaging in conversations about controversial issues? Will opinions casually offered be used later to influence decisions about retention or promotion? Must African American workers withhold our opinions or stifle disagreement about the issues for which we feel passion? Working while black sometimes requires walking a tightrope, with less freedom than others have to simply "be."

A week after the Sherrod case broke, another "reverse racism" story hit the news. *Essence* magazine, the black-founded but now Time Warner owned black women's magazine, hired a white fashion director, much to the chagrin of several *Essence* staff alumnae, who took to the airwaves to talk about it. It was refreshing to see a group of brilliant black women in respectful disagreement about *Essence*'s hiring of Elliana Placas, and their dialogue provided useful lessons about segregation in the fashion industry. Again, there was the smug white charge of "reverse racism" when conscientious African American women dared even speak to their disappointment. And, again, there was the possibility of heated watercooler conversation. Since the news is never divorced from the workplace, conversations often have long-term and subtle consequences for those working while black.

Michelle Johnson brings her unique background as an attorney, diversity expert, and motivational speaker to a broad range of the issues that affect African American workers, from hair and attire and the electronic media and social networking to cultural competency, alliances and relationships, attitude, and legal remedies for discrimination. Chock-full of examples, wisdom, and insight, this book provides a useful perch from which to consider the ways the workplace has changed and the many ways that it has not changed for African Americans.

Just like driving while black, walking while black, and even voting while black, working while black carries a special tax that African American workers pay wittingly and unwittingly. Michelle

Johnson hopes for the day when the tax will no longer be levied, when we will, perhaps, live in a post-racial world. In the interim, though, her witty, wise, and hopeful book encourages African American workers to seek success, surtax notwithstanding. Even with the "black tax," there are no victims in Michelle Johnson's working-while-black world. Her positive energy and her assertion that we each own our experiences as employees make this book quite an exciting read.

—Dr. Julianne Malveaux
Economist, president of Bennett College for Women

PREFACE

∎

I'VE ALWAYS BEEN a big fan of nonfiction books, even as a kid, and whenever a new and revised edition of a book I've already bought comes out, I'm usually skeptical, asking myself if anything all that remarkable has happened since the author wrote the original version to require an updated edition.

But in writing an advice book for black workers on how to navigate Corporate America, I couldn't have ever predicted how much would change between 2002, when I began writing this book, and 2010, as I completed the revised edition: a nationally unknown black man with a Muslim-sounding name would run for president of the United States, not only receive the Democratic nomination but win the entire election, and move his black wife and children into the White House; a brutal recession would turn this country on its head in terms of jobs, money, and basic security; social networking sites would give not just black people but an entire country new and popular avenues to be stupid and broadcast details of their personal business, along with providing photos. And those are just the key changes.

For me personally, the big change was leaving Corporate America and one of the most high-status professions in the country—the practice of law—because I found much more fulfillment in helping people work out diversity issues before they had to sue rather than afterward. The transition hasn't always been easy, and it's certainly not more lucrative, but it has been infinitely more rewarding in ways I wouldn't trade for all the law books sold in America.

As part of that transition, I've spent my share of time on the road listening to the experiences and problems of black employees as I've traveled the country for book tours and speaking engagements related to *Working While Black*. I never cease to be amazed at how much more common the issues I wrote about were than even I knew while writing the book.

My aim in writing the book was to focus on the universal issues that faced black employees, ranging from getting a job to keeping a job to leaving a job—a cradle-to-grave advice book, so to speak. I had no idea just how well I tapped into that, as people seemed really hungry to know that others were having similar experiences. I had more than one sistah literally cry on me as she explained issues she was going through at work.

One of the most powerful impressions made on me was by a young woman with, let's just say, a first name that would completely identify her as African American to any employer who saw it on a resume. She burst out in tears when I suggested that she adopt a nickname and start putting that on her resume. She cried because she was relieved to have another black person not accuse her of being a sellout because she didn't want her name triggering prejudices before she even got her foot in the door.

Sometimes I would be the one in tears, when I got unexpected e-mails from people who had just read my book and found that it was particularly helpful. In fact, it was the e-mail from a young brother out of California who told me how much the book assisted him, both when he graduated from college and as he has started his career, that prompted me to approach my publisher about updating the book since so much was changing in the world for blacks.

As I said in the original edition, sometimes the biggest stress reliever in the workplace as a black employee is just knowing that you aren't crazy and that other people are having the same experiences. I know that as a black employee for all the years before writing that book, even when I talked to friends about things going on at work, I thought it was just me. Or just the individuals I worked for. That's one of the reasons I went into employment law, because I just knew there was some piece I was missing. It turns out there was no missing piece, just people being people with the same stories, situations, feelings, and reactions happening all over the country. Different names, different workplaces, different cities and towns, same story.

I know that the universal nature of what I've written about is what makes the book—both the original and this revised edition—continue to be relevant. One day "working while black" will be an outdated concept, but as any black working knows, not for a long, long time.

—Michelle T. Johnson
Michelle@MichelleTJohnson.com

INTRODUCTION

■

Race is probably one of the trickiest subjects two people can talk about. It's particularly tricky when the two people are of two different races, because their perspectives are so ingrained that one can't really get inside the other's head.

That's why the times we live in are so amazingly contradictory. We can sit in front of a tiny little screen, click a few buttons, type a few words, and have access to information from the other side of the globe in a matter of seconds; yet, as a black person in America, you could spend hours at a party talking with a white person about the reasons why it is acceptable for black people to use the *n*-word but not whites. That is because *information* and *understanding* are not synonymous.

Working While Black is a black person's guide to employment in the white work world. That seems like a simple topic, and yet it implies and promises so much. It implies that in a few easy steps, I can tell you how to navigate the work world as a black person. Well, I can't—I'm still navigating that myself.

One thing I can tell you is that being a black person in the white work world requires internal fortitude. There are no easy steps. There are no simple answers. Each person is completely different, each job raises different challenges, and each step of the process calls for different skills. In an ideal world, this book would simply be about employment, and a person of any race could pick it up and get every concept in it. It would just be a book about how to pick a career, how to get a job, and how to keep and enjoy a job. There wouldn't be any special considerations. But this is the real world, and so there are.

I was told that this book shouldn't be too negative because young blacks would suffer from a lack of motivation. What my well-meaning white friend did not get is that motivation is not the issue. Black people are going to be highly motivated in whatever we do. We're going to reach for the stars and try to get ours no matter what, because that is who we are. We're human, and we want to live well and do well, too. Blacks get inundated with the same mass advertising that white America gets—taunting us to want more, buy more, own better. Most people buying this book aren't going to succumb to a life of crime or purposeful unemployment just because the working life is hard.

A book, like a life, is a work in progress—especially when you are writing a book about something that touches your life profoundly, both personally and professionally. While I worked on this book I tried to focus on specific points, and my mind became flooded with half-forgotten memories from my own life addressing what I was trying to say. Some detail from a case that supported my point would come back to me, or I'd recall a situation in a friend's life that was particularly illustrative.

In the same week I sent the manuscript of the first edition to my editor, one of my closest friends, a black professional, was fired from her job somewhat suddenly, and, in my job as an attorney, I sat through the depositions of four black employees suing their company for race discrimination.

During the same week I was reading a book that suggested we attract every experience and condition we have in life because of our feelings, including particular issues such as illness, tragedy, and discrimination. The point about attracting everything that happens to us, good or bad, was a bit surreal. The concept went against everything I've ever thought about bad things happening to good people and yet totally supported it, too. For example, while my initial emotional reaction to my friend being fired was to wail about how terribly unfair it was and how screwed I felt she had been, she was the first to say that while she was nervous about finding a job in a stalled economy, she was relieved to some degree because of how much she hated her job. So, in a sense, she was an example of how deep-rooted negativity about a situation can attract the one thing you think you don't want.

As I sat in on the plaintiffs' depositions in the case, I was amazed at the degree of fresh, sincere passion these people expressed in recounting events that had happened years before. Even though the supervisors they complained about were no longer with the company, even though most of the plaintiffs had moved on to better jobs, and even though all of them sounded like they had good lives outside of work, they still swelled with anger and indignation as they talked about their experiences.

The concept of attracting experience is equally relevant here. While these people may not have deserved bad treatment at the hands of either illegal discrimination or garden-variety (yet legal) racism, in some part they were equal parties to their pain. I don't mean they were responsible for being on the receiving end of their alleged discrimination, but that they were choosing to stay stuck in the pain of the experience by constantly reliving it through the lawsuit. It's like the Buddhist concept: pain is a necessary part of life, but suffering is optional.

It becomes a very tough statement to make, because it seems as if we are letting our oppressors off the hook. Failing to blame, accuse, and attack bad behavior feels as if you're endorsing it. I think this is one of the reasons why blacks (in general) and whites (in general) have such different views of affirmative action. Many blacks, in supporting affirmative action, are saying, "Hey, white folks, you don't need to be off the hook yet. The playing field hasn't even begun to be evened, and to say otherwise is to let you get away with all you've done, all you're still doing, and all you're going to do." The whites who oppose affirmative action, on the other hand, are saying, "Look, black people, you can't have it both ways. You say you don't want decisions to be about race when it hurts you, but you're willing to let decisions be about race when it helps you. That's not fair to the hard-working, innocent white people who have not committed any wrongs."

I wrote this book because I've had the full-time job and joy of being black for over forty years. For eight of those years, I was a full-time lawyer, mostly practicing in employment law.

As an employee, I wish I had a five-dollar bill for every time I have had to examine how a comment, decision, or something else done by a white coworker or boss might have had negative implications. I've even had conversations with white coworkers who also found themselves scratching their heads, puzzled over the stupidity of a white boss who left behind racial tracks. Sometimes that Monday morning conversation, question, or analysis involved some backstabbing maneuver done by a member of our own race. Yep, I mean black-on-black crime in the workplace. Every time that little problem comes up, your fellow brother or sister's knife seems just a little sharper and plunges a little deeper into your heart.

Race is the little angel/devil that constantly hovers over your shoulder in the work world if you're a black person. If you're particularly blessed or lucky, there may be entire weeks of your working life where you can get so immersed in the pleasures and satisfaction your job gives you that you can have a fade-out and not consider racial implications. I don't mean fade out and forget you're black but rather not be any more aware of being black than you are when you're at home, at a family reunion, or driving in a car by yourself.

Whites really don't want to hear this. I think it is because part of them feels guilty, and another part of them gets angry for feeling guilty about something that they don't think they should feel guilty about because it's not their fault, and the cycle starts again. Oh well. This book isn't about white people's responses. It is about black empowerment in a world where we do have to deal with white people's responses.

I had my first job at age fourteen. Because I was blessed with a womanly physique (to put it tactfully), the fast-food restaurant manager didn't blink when I said I was sixteen years old. I honestly can't remember if it was the manager's suggestion or my own to leave, but I know I didn't last in that first job for more than three weeks. What I do distinctly remember about the job was my strong belief that a person needed to be given two packets of syrup when he or she ordered pancakes for breakfast. The manager insisted that a person only needed one. Even then, I had an oddball sense of integrity. I lied about my age to get the job (my first and only resume fraud), but I was willing to lose the job because I didn't think it was fair that people found out only after they got home that they had way more pancakes than syrup.

But the job you have at fourteen, to make money for stuff you don't really need, is a far different reality than the job you have at twenty-one, when you live two thousand miles from home and your college degree is so new it sparkles. At twenty-one you not only have rent, food, and student loans at stake, you also have ego. Therefore, when your first job out of college ends with your boss, in my case an East Coast city editor, telling another reporter that he didn't like me because "she doesn't act grateful enough to be here," well, you know it's going to be a long and bumpy ride. Actually, in that particular case, it was a short and bumpy ride.

I learned a lot from that experience. I learned that no matter how good you are at what you do, if you've got a white-boy attitude in a black woman's body, there's going to be a lot of clinking and clashing at some point. I also learned that how you succeed in the workplace is often about how you manage the workplace itself as much as how well you do your job.

When I buy a good self-help book, I hope it gives me a fresh look at a particular part of my life. But I don't expect a book to be a substitute for my own decision-making process. If you're reading this book, you're probably a black person who's working. You have a job, you want a job, or you've just lost a job and you want to know if you're holding it together right. Since every job is so distinctly different, you should use this book as a guide to trusting your own inner light. For example, for a black person, getting a job as a nurse's aide in Tupelo, Mississippi, will be handled differently from getting one in Boise, Idaho. While most of the essentials are the same—the application and interview processes—the nuances might be completely different. The supervisor in Boise might be indifferent to whether you are black or not, while the top dog in Tupelo, because of his history with blacks, might be a straight-up racist. While this book may provide some guidelines on what to do about getting past the racist, only the person applying for the job knows whether that would be in his or her best interest anyway.

How you start is how you finish. In starting off any job or job situation with questions instead of assumptions, you end up with more peace of mind and have a better foundation for your decisions. This book doesn't try to come up with the Holy Grail of answers. The goal is to help you increase your awareness. While certain realities might not change, increased awareness might help you make better on-the-spot decisions when you're at work. On many days, the decision may be nothing more than choosing not to internalize a dose of someone else's bad behavior.

Knowing your intention is in your hands. Choosing your options is in your hands. Helping you to evaluate your options is the aim of this book. Among these pages you'll find information on these topics:

- Why blacks need to think of the workplace differently and with a strategy
- How to decide where to work (the internal process you need to go through)
- How to get the first job, or how to career hop (once you decide what you want, how to get it)

- The importance of language and grooming style in the workplace
- Alliances in the workplace
- Fitting in without selling out
- Attitude issues that arise in the workplace if you're black
- Considering legal options when problems arise
- What happens when you get fired or quit
- How to be a healthy, happy person inside and outside of work

There are employment manuals, and there are books that describe the sociological experience of being a black person in America. *Working While Black* aims to combine both—it's an employment guide that acknowledges the average black reader's frustration about working in a society where equality is a promise but not a reality.

WORKING
WHILE BLACK

1

THE 15 PERCENT DIFFERENCE

■

Life is hard for blacks before they get their first job. Whether we went to a private school or a public school or an all-black school or a mostly white school, if we've dealt with whites in any capacity, being different and having different experiences isn't new to us. Today's average sixteen-year-old black may deal with it less than his grandparents did when they were young, but *less than* is not the same as *not at all*.

I think many whites, including (ironically) even liberal whites, don't get that even though our experiences as black people can be 85 percent the same as white people, some days that 15 percent difference is the only difference we feel.[1] Technically

---

1. Please understand that the phrase "15 percent difference" is neither scientific nor factual. It's merely shorthand to address the fact that as a black employee in white America, most of the objective things you deal with are not race issues. Also, please do not feel that I'm saying that the 15 percent difference is only a minor aspect of the work experience. For some people, it's the most influential aspect of who they are. For example, Condoleezza Rice had to worry less about the 15 percent difference when she was contemplating foreign

much of this book will apply to any worker regardless of race, but that 15 percent difference for blacks is going to put just a little bit of a spin on the rest of our day.

For example, applying for a job is applying for a job—no matter what your color or race, you need to fill out an application or submit a resume and go through some formalized process to actually get the job offer. But at some point, there are those 15 percent issues that put just a little twist on our experience. For example, if the receptionist who takes your application has had bad experiences with blacks, your resume may end up at the bottom of the pile, meaning you never even get the interview. Therefore, that 15 percent can be the difference between you getting through the door or not or the difference between you being happy or miserable once you get through that door.

This book aims to do a couple of things. One is to address the 85 percent commonality, and two is to give you helpful advice, tips, and perspective for when that 15 percent pops up. I know that many times just knowing that I'm not alone is enough to get me through an experience or put perspective on a puzzling situation.

---

policy in Russia than she did with her first job out of college. It's not that Ms. Rice doesn't deal with the 15 percent issues anymore, they just play out differently when you and the president of the United States have watched football games together. I'm sure that when Condoleezza talks behind closed doors with her girls about earlier jobs, she could write a book about how her 15 percent issues played out less than positively. Jesse Jackson, on the other hand, has to constantly factor in the black perspective in what he does just by the nature of his particular career path. Condoleezza is no less black than Jesse. It's just that on most days, as one of the single most important black people in government, she got to leverage her 15 percent differently than Jesse does. One could say that when you're a leader in the civil rights movement, your 15 percent is actually 100 percent.

When I was in law school, many of the other blacks I met there wanted to go into civil rights law because they wanted to make a difference in the lives of black people. While civil rights law is a great area, I personally feel that black people make a difference wherever we are and whatever we do. We pay taxes. We have wills and estates when we die. We get divorced. We have car accidents. We buy and sell companies. In other words, as blacks we have the power to influence the whole world. One black person changes the dynamic just by being in the room; so yes, while it is important to be at the forefront of civil rights, all these other areas of the law need us, too. One of the reasons our people marched for civil rights and put their bodies, lives, and livelihoods at risk was so that no door would be closed to us. One of my favorite quotes from Martin Luther King Jr. speaks to this issue:

> *If you are called to be a street sweeper, sweep streets even as Michelangelo painted, or Beethoven composed music, or Shakespeare wrote poetry. Sweep streets so well that all the hosts of heaven and earth will pause to say, "Here lived a great street sweeper who did his job well."*

Notice that King didn't say if you're called to be a doctor, lawyer, or chemical engineer. King said a street sweeper because he knew that it was a humble job but one that still required heart to do it well. I'd like to think that one of King's points was that the struggle for equality was not just for black Americans to get the best jobs in our society but rather for each of us to get any job or opportunity in our society that was best suited to our individual dream.

Maybe that's why it is easier to be a black civil rights attorney than a black tax attorney in a large, white law firm, or maybe it's easier to be a teacher in an inner-city school district rather than the headmaster at a hoity-toity East Coast school. But each person has the right to deal with that 15 percent difference however he or she chooses. Maybe the black tax attorney gets her rocks off from calculating tax exemptions for the wealthy. Maybe the black headmaster loves a more extravagant lifestyle than a public school salary can offer. Therefore, when these 15 percent issues come up, it may all be worth it. It should be, because none of us can avoid it anyway.

Let me repeat: *none of us can avoid it anyway.* No matter what path you choose, if another person can look at you and tell you're black, that will mold your experience with that person from that point forward. Notice I didn't say it will negatively mold it, just that it will.

Do You Instinctively Aim to Survive, Strive, or Thrive?

My observation, from thirty years of working, eight years of practicing employment law, and several years of being a diversity expert, remains that black folks have roughly one of three instinctive agendas in the workplace. And this delineation is true whether we're talking minimum wage, blue-collar, just plain-ol'-shirt-on-your-back-when-you-go-to-work-in-the-morning-collar, or white-collar professional.[2]

---

2. My classification does not cover artists, athletes, or entrepreneurs, or even blacks who work for other blacks. (However, I do like black opera singer Leontyne Price's advice: "Be

Working while black requires you to have a mental awareness, a psychological game plan, so to speak. You've got to know if you're in it just to survive, if you're in it to strive to get ahead, or if you're in it to thrive, be your natural brown self, and make the white folks move to your rhythm instead of constantly having to adapt to theirs.

There is no particular mentality that is best for every black person. Every job change, every career choice, and maybe even every change in supervision might force you to make a drastic shift in whether you're in the game to survive, to strive, or to thrive; however, no matter what your initial motivation or instinct, you can always choose to be a driver, creating your own destiny.

I've created these categories based on my experiences in the working world. For me, there is no value judgment attached to being in the workplace as a survivor, a striver, or a thriver. We've all been visitors to each place at some point in our working careers. Some people settle into the lifelong comfort zone of being survivors. Some people were ambitious from the first step they took as toddlers, so they will be diehard strivers. Other people come out of the womb pushing their mama's limits, and those thrivers spend the rest of their lives doing the same to everyone else as well.

---

black, shine, aim high.") Now while blacks who work for other blacks have similar issues and dynamics as blacks who work for whites, this situation still raises other issues. For example, a friend of mine, an attorney who once worked for an all-black law firm, and I used to trade many a long-distance phone call with stories about who had it rougher. In our game of "who's got it worse," we would compare insanities of kowtowing to white folks versus working for black folks who were trippin' because they pulled the strings. We jokingly decided to stop playing that game when we realized we were always going to stalemate, since at the end of the day we both worked for bosses who left us needing to have this conversation in the first place.

A *survivor* is there for the paycheck and lives his or her work life like a duck floating on smooth waters. Someone who is trying to survive wants to stay under the radar. His goal is to not draw attention to himself or do anything other than work, collect the paycheck, and get out the door when the clock strikes whenever. Survivors do not like negative attention. They do not like positive attention. They don't like any attention and are indifferent to the desire to distinguish themselves.

There is a black woman I've known all of my adult life. She's been my mentor, my boss, my guide, my lookout, my savior, and always my friend. Years before I knew I would become a lawyer or write a book (or even believed I could do either), she was the original person to teach me by example how to be a survivor, a striver, and the ultimate thriver. Now she's in her late fifties, and she has one of the best descriptions I can think of for what it is to be in the workplace on the survivor agenda. As she puts it now, "You get to the point where you're just in it for the health insurance."

Being a survivor as a black person in the workplace can mean different things to different people at different points in their lives. It's the person who knows this particular boss can't stand her and is looking for any excuse to eliminate her job. It's the person who is working the only job he can find that pays more than five dollars an hour because he has a family to support. It's the person who has put his thirty years in and knows he's gone as far as he is going to get in an organization before retirement hits.

A *striver* likes the radar screen. She wants to be on it, but only if it's a good thing. If she's lucky, she aims to run the radar screen one day, even if no black employee in the history of her workplace has ever done it before. The black striver wants acclaim, promotions, and success. She wants to play the game because she believes she can win. She doesn't mind hearing about glass ceilings because, in her mind, glass can be broken. She sees to the top and doesn't care if she bumps her head or gets scraped on the climb.

A striver is one who believes that the system works and believes that benefits come by following the system. Look at newly minted black college graduates—that is probably where you are going to see the prototype of a striver. Strivers believe that an education, a plan, and pure, raw ambition will make the difference. These folks strive forward, strive to the top, strive to get a huge slice of what their parents may not necessarily have had a shot at.

The *thriver* is the black person who not only dances to his or her own beat but also creates his or her own rhythm. Thrivers don't care about the radar screen because they figure it was invented to track other people anyway, not them. Thrivers are the ones who are going to dress the way they want and talk the way they want; it is not an option for them to get in by trying to fit in.

Thrivers are easy to spot. The thriver is the black person who puts the white folks either a little or a lot on edge. White bosses assume (sometimes mistakenly, sometimes not) that if any black employee might file a complaint or sue them, it will be the thriver. Of course, bosses don't refer to them as thrivers—more likely they're called "troublemakers" or "the mouthy ones" or "the ones with an attitude problem." A thriver may just be the person referred to by name with an accompanying eye roll. Success for the thriver isn't necessarily the goal the way it is for a striver, although some are quite successful. Some are loud. Others are offbeat. The truly lucky ones work at places where they are not

perceived as loud or different or ghetto or crazy or troublemakers or any of the other negative labels that often get attached to
blacks who operate by their own internal agendas.

My woman friend whom I mentioned earlier as an example
of someone in the survivor mode as she cruises toward the next
stage of her life was an unabashed thriver when I first met her
fifteen years ago. She was the person who taught me how to have
a "F—k You Fund" at all times so that if your employer ever
tripped too hard, you could say "F—k you," quit without a job,
and have a three-month cushion to find a job where you won't
get disrespected. I can't say I've always had a fund that size, but
I did inherit the attitude.

The Proof Is in the Pudding

Being black in America isn't simple, and going to work every day
as a black person is not for the fainthearted. A few years ago, I
made up a saying. It is a silly, nonsensical expression that I liked,
and it's stuck with a few friends: "The proof is in the pudding,
not the pudding mix." That was my standard way of saying look
to someone's results, not just what she says about how she is going
to get the results. Being black in America isn't simple, but it is
simple to constantly evaluate your circumstances to make sure
you're achieving what you want. That's the pudding—coming up
with a work experience that makes you feel happy and successful. Unless you are rich, work for yourself, or are a homemaker,
you have to work for someone else. Let's face it, even if you work
for yourself or you work for other blacks, you still need to figure
out how to deal with whites in the work context, whether you're

dealing with customers, clients, vendors, employees, the government—you name it. The proof is in the pudding, not the pudding mix.

This book doesn't provide fill-in-the-blank answers. (I wish I had those kinds of answers because I could have used them myself over the years.) This book attempts to ask good questions, outline common-sense scenarios, and provide real-life solutions. My division between blacks on whether they are in it to survive, strive, or thrive is by no means definitive. It's just a shorthand way of explaining the different approaches that black employees take when managing the workplace jungle.

A white male friend of mine recently talked about a mutual friend of ours who is a white woman and disabled. She has been in a wheelchair her entire adult life. My male friend commented that in terms of life difficulties, it is probably harder for our friend than for those faced with racial discrimination because her limitations are physical. I pointed out that in some ways it's probably the opposite, because ultimately, as difficult as her situation is, no one is going to argue with her about whether she can go up stairs or through a door. Her disability is a physical fact, so she doesn't have to explain or doubt herself. Ultimately, no one blames her for being upset if she can't enter a building or use a bathroom. When you're talking limitations relating to race, you never know what's really going on (unless a person uses the *n*-word, which is something even the stupidest white person knows not to do in public anymore). Sometimes you can feel resistance, insensitivity, or futility, but you can't see it or prove it. The existence of a physical limitation doesn't have to be explained. When a person is blind, for example, and walks into another person accidentally, no one speculates whether the person is just clumsy or has a defective cane. But if black people say they received bad service at a restaurant because of their race, some white people usually rush in to offer their own bad experiences at the same restaurant or speculate that maybe the server might have been having a bad day. My point is not that it is better to be physically disabled than black (and I won't touch on the difficulties of being both), but that to be black in working white America is to have your experiences constantly negated and challenged by whites who can't, or don't want to, understand. Part of this understanding is to remember that if the average black person is wrong some of the time when he says race is an issue, then that means some of the time he's right. If there is anything more stressful to a black person than sensing something is about race when you can't really know for sure, it's having a white person act like you're blameworthy to even consider whether race is an issue.

If you're a reasonable person, you know that just because you feel something is off does not necessarily mean that it is about race. But sometimes you just don't know. Again, that 15 percent factor constantly creeps up.

Most of the time, you never really know. Hopefully, what you get from reading this book is the comfort of knowing that it is OK to not always know. And on those occasions when you wonder, questions are good, because the path to finding out what you need to know can be as useful as the answer you come up with.

The advice-giving books (also known as "self-help" and "how-to") still leap off the shelves. We all want to know the exact steps to take to make our lives better. I know I've bought several dozen in my life on how to lose weight, gain a relationship, obtain a job, unload a bad habit, and more. I'm a particular fan of the "Complete Idiot" and "For Dummies" guides. A relative of mine used to tease me for buying those books, saying he refused to buy a book that said he was an idiot. I explained that he missed the point. The purpose of a good self-help book is to take you back to yourself and the beginning of your knowledge about something. It's not that any of us is an idiot or stupid about anything. Essentially, we're all to some degree ignorant, innocent, or naive about some aspect of our lives.

A baby struggles to breathe on day one and then gets that skill down pat. Then walking becomes the skill to master, then riding a bike. At some point the baby, now an adult, learns to drive a car. In other words, life is a series of lessons to find ways to propel ourselves forward.

Again, the bottom line does end up being about not allowing yourself to be a victim even when others try to engage in victimizing behavior. That's why while almost all blacks may instinctively operate from the gut level of being survivors, strivers, or thrivers, ultimately, what we should all aim to be are drivers—drivers of our lives, our career paths, and our destinies. Whether you run a forklift or you run the financial division of a Fortune 500 company, you want to be the driving force behind how you got where you are, the nature of your experiences while you are there, and whether you want to continue to stay or move forward to something else.

The thing to remember is that all black employees deal with that 15 percent difference, and it can be some comfort to know you're not alone. The key is how you choose to deal with it.

The 15 Percent Difference Today

That 15 percent difference is that feeling, that gut instinct that you usually can't support with facts, that makes you think that being black is a source of contention in your workplace. Maybe it's a difference in how you feel your supervisors treat you compared to your coworkers who aren't black. Maybe it's the subtle comments that your coworkers make about things at work or in the news that put you on red alert. Maybe it's the decisions that top management make over and over again that give the impression that your being black will be a detriment to your upward mobility.

Whether it's based on fact or fear or it's a carryover from the last three jobs you worked where it was an issue, it's a difference that haunts you and permeates everything you do in a way that probably only another black person can really get. That's why during a good period or under a particularly good employer, that difference may feel like 2 percent, while during a really rocky period where there is no trust for the people you work with or for, that difference can feel like 80 percent.

Never was that difference more profoundly felt, most likely, for any black employee in Corporate America than when Senator Barack Obama ran for president. If it didn't start when he announced his candidacy, it probably kicked in when he won the Iowa caucus and there was a collective feeling of, "Oh my God, a black man is being taken seriously in running for president? Hey now!"

Even though Obama's campaign technically had nothing to do with the jobs of most black Americans, it in fact had everything to do with them. That's part of what that 15 percent difference is about—having anything major concerning blacks at work or in society make you feel like you're walking around with a big spotlight shining right on you at all times. At the very least, it might make you feel like there will be something jumping out at you from around the next workplace corner.

Even in workplaces were most of the people were heavily leaning toward voting for Obama—placards, posters, and T-shirts happily and openly spotted the workplace—the work experience of blacks was seriously altered whether they wanted to admit to it or not. How could it not when every newspaper article, every television news story, and every radio rant or report focused heavily on Barack Obama's race? His race. Your race. Interchangeable realities for some.

I mean, honestly, how many conversations did every black employee find him- or herself subjected to in 2008 about Obama where deep down he or she felt like it was all about being a representative for the race? Even when the conversation wasn't about race, almost any conversation initiated about Obama by a white person left the black employee feeling even more self-conscious than usual. Some were lucky if it was just left at self-conscious rather than irritated, angry, and annoyed by ignorance and presumptions.

The whole premise of this book, despite the discomfort that many nonblacks may have with this notion, is that blacks have to navigate Corporate America differently because they are a visible minority with a distinct history. Although it differs from person to person and job to job, the bottom line is that blacks, like any other visible minority, have certain commonalities with each other that distinguish their path in Corporate America from the majority. In simpler terms, we always stand out. And in standing out, we battle stereotypes and preconceptions.

Yes, of course, as so many people like to immediately jump to, it's better than it was twenty years ago, forty years ago. But most of us aren't content with "better than." We're still aiming for the day when race is irrelevant, when it's noticed with the same level of interest or emotion as noting whether someone is left- or right-handed.

But that's not the case yet.

That's why, during the presidential campaign, blacks had to listen to watercooler talk and coffee-pot discussions dissecting every aspect of Barack Obama the Black Man. Every criticism, every personal attack, every question about his religious leanings, his parents, his wife, his preachers, his teachers, his friends, and his neighborhoods got interpreted by every armchair psychologist out there. Hell, we even had to hear stories and commentaries on how he would put up a basketball hoop at the White House if he won. For some, he might as well have had the campaign slogan, "A chicken in every pot and Colt 45 malt liquor to go with it."

And guess what? When that happens in front of you as a black person and you get drawn into a discussion, far more often than not it's a stressor. It's always a stressor when you have to educate white folks along with doing your job, even when you're educating white people you like. I remember in particular that when the Reverend Wright controversy came up, I couldn't begin to keep track of the number of conversations I personally had schooling white people on the differing dynamics of black churches, the legitimacy of some of what Wright said, or the context for the things he said that I didn't even agree with. I did it because I felt as if black people were indirectly being attacked by the media machine, and I wasn't going to have that in my little slice of the world.

Ultimately, the election of Barack Obama, while a great source of enduring and pervasive pride, took an immeasurable toll on the blacks in the workplace who constantly have to explain and/or tolerate all aspects of being black. Some blacks would consider it a small price to pay if it got enough whites properly informed. But I still say that along the way, it was stressful and exhausting.

So even if you were completely thrilled that Obama won, that's great. But you were probably still irritated at the number of news stories and comments from people that America was now "post-racial" because enough white people voted for a black man to get elected president. (To paraphrase the great Cornel West, why wasn't America post-racial all the years that people of color had been voting for white folks?)

Part of this post-racial nonsense was that many in America wanted to believe the slate was clean on American racism toward blacks. One of the frequent comments heard was "Can affirmative action end now that a black man is president?" As if one deserving black man winning one election meant that all the rest of America no longer discriminated on the basis of race.

Unfortunately, once Obama won the presidency, the increased feeling of stress and attention to race didn't go away. Yes, there was a high for many blacks on Inauguration Day. Even making fun of Aretha Franklin's hat showed that more blacks than ever actually paid attention. It was beyond surreal to see the footage of the First Family moving into the White House. But the honeymoon pretty much ended there.

Once Obama began to really govern in the first year, blacks found the feeling of scrutiny kicking in even more intensely than it did when he ran for office. When the black person actually gets the job or does the crime or makes the news splash, you always have that uncomfortable sense of feeling like a representative for the black race. You know that not every white person you work with feels that way, but you can't help but feel it anyway.

Other groups—other ethnicities, gay people, employees with disabilities—feel the same way, bearing the weight of all other famous people's transgressions and disappointments. That's the flip side of the coin of feeling pride for successes. Because whether we like it or not, as blacks in the workplace, at some level we always feel that we're on trial—like we have to prove both individually and as a race that we're not the stereotype that we know some walk around believing that we are. And unfortunately in the constant trial that some of us don't even want to admit to being on, the evidence is usually the life of every black person who hits the news. If nothing else, that's what Barack Obama symbolized for a lot of black folks. He was Exhibit A that we could be highly educated, erudite, moral, and able to hold our own with any white person on the planet while still being all the way black and happy to be nappy.

On the other hand, there is one black celebrity that average black Americans probably didn't find themselves much identifying with or supporting in the court of public opinion. That was mainly because Tiger Woods committed the ultimate sin in the minds of black Americans: he essentially disavowed being black. For coming up with the term "Cablinasian" and making one personal decision after another that demonstrated his lukewarm connection to the black race, blacks allowed Tiger his distance.

Frankly, I think we blacks would be better served if we stopped overidentifying with every black person whom we don't personally know, allowing ourselves to be lumped together with all other black people, regardless of whether the other blacks are doing things worthy of pride or worthy of explanation and defense. I proclaim this knowing that it is in some ways asking the impossible of us as a culture.

During the election, a white man named Andrew M. Manis, an associate professor of history at Macon State College in Georgia, wrote a widely circulated column in which he chastised whites for being the ones who couldn't "get over" race in our society and for blaming blacks for that problem. He pointed out that whites needed to hold other whites accountable for racist words and actions. My favorite line from his column was his question, "How long before we white people get over our bitter resentments about being demoted to the status of equality with nonwhites?"

I'm not a big fan of forwarding things to people by e-mail, but that column I forwarded to several people. A few of my white friends told me that they were very offended by the premise of the column, because they didn't appreciate being lumped together with racist white people.

If you're a friend of mine, you know I calls it as I sees it. I told my offended white friends that I understood exactly where they were coming from but that Manis was simply doing what black leaders have been doing since Moses was a baby: admonishing the people in a community who know better to take responsibility for putting their feet down when they see the bad behavior of others. In other words, I said that whites generally have the luxury of not thinking of themselves as being associated with the bad behavior of other whites. A white person doesn't say, "Oh damn, I hope he's not white!" when she hears the tease for the evening news about the latest serial killer or thieving CEO or politician caught in a sex scandal. While whites may be accustomed to being accused of racism by nonwhites, they generally aren't called upon by other whites to collectively take responsibility for the bad behavior of their race. Blacks are used to being assaulted with collective guilt and responsibility—and just like my white friends rejected being put in that position, it will be nice when blacks reject it too.

2

WHERE TO BE A BLACK EMPLOYEE IN WHITE AMERICA

■

Richard clerked for a law firm in a Southern city the summer between his second and third year of law school in the mid-1990s. The clerkship was for one of those huge firms that you see in the movies. For a law student, a summer clerkship is typically the ticket to a job when you graduate.

Although Richard loved the money he was making that summer—more money than he knew people even could make in a week—he didn't like the fact that he was the only black summer clerk. But Richard chose to just be happy to be nappy and to take it all in stride. There were black attorneys and other blacks employed in the firm, so he figured if he could just get the job in the end, well, it would all work out.

All summer long, Richard worked his butt off. He wrote tons of memos, researched for hours on end, and was generally known as a bright and friendly guy. In addition to doing the work, he also did a big part of the extras that were required—schmoozing with all the white people. He did the dinner parties and the canoe trip and the lunches and the barbecues. He even did the country-and-western party with a smile on his face.

Richard put the emphasis on the work. He knocked himself out paying attention to every little detail so that when the summer was over he would get the call offering him a job. Fast forward to August when he got his end-of-the-summer review from one of the partners.

"Great work product." Check. "Outstanding work ethic." Check. "Overall, one of the best clerks this summer." Heading to a home run. "There's just one little concern, however, Richard." Uh-oh. "One of the partners who went on the firm-sponsored canoe trip was concerned about the fact that you made some remark about being the only black person in a hundred-mile radius of the town where the canoe trip was located."

Richard suddenly knew what the phrase "seeing red" meant. He had never had a truly violent impulse in his life, but if ever there were a time he felt like busting heads, it was at that moment. He sat there while the partner inquired about his ability to work with whites, report to whites, deal with whites. Richard couldn't believe that in the 1990s he was dealing with this in an evaluation as if this were a legitimate issue.

As a black person in America, working for a living is pretty much the one thing in life you're going to do. Like brushing your teeth in the morning, it's not something you can do once and expect it to cover you for the rest of your life. Working is something you pretty much have to keep doing. Working presents a lifetime of decisions and choices.

The concept of choices does not just start with the first job either. It used to be common for people, particularly blacks who had limited choices to begin with, to get a job when they graduated from high school or college and stay at that job until they retired. For most black families, because slavery and Jim Crow are a part of our legacy, making a good decision about a job used to involve no more analysis than asking if it paid well and had benefits. If you came from one of the privileged Talented Tenth type of families, then you might be pressured to join a profession such as law or medicine or pushed to own a business. (Black intellectual W. E. B. DuBois coined the phrase "Talented Tenth" in the early 1900s to describe the top 10 percent of Negroes who should seek higher education rather than the industrial training opportunities espoused by Booker T. Washington.) Starting in the 1960s, with the advent of better (but not perfect) laws and expanding social consciousness, opportunities improved, and so did the range of choices for black Americans.

Richard's example may not be typical of what happens to a black legal intern, but it does show that as the stakes go up, so does the range of choices, problems, and opportunities. The last thing Richard expected in his evaluation was to have to defend himself against allegations that he noticed he was black. Nevertheless, with more heat than he had ever shown during that long, hot summer of working, Richard asked the partner if he was interrogating the more than a dozen white clerks on their ability to get along with blacks and other ethnic groups. Richard asked if the other clerks' performances would be held hostage to their skills in dealing with black judges, black opposing counsel, black clients, or black witnesses.

Richard ended his evaluation by telling the partner that if Big Southern Fried Law Firm wanted to hire blacks who could forget their race the second they got to work, then he wasn't someone they should hire. As his parting shot, Richard stated that instead of questioning the lone black clerk about his ability to get along with whites because of one comment, maybe the partners ought to question why they felt it fun to take an annual firm-sponsored canoe trip to an area well known for the presence of the Ku Klux Klan.

In the end, Richard got the job offer, worked for the firm for a few years, and left when he figured out that his gut instincts about really being able to succeed in that firm were correct—that his skin color would make it harder to make partner there. He had wanted to believe that the anonymous partner's obvious racism was an aberration. Instead, what Richard found out was that while blatant racism was not common, Richard was way too tall for the glass ceiling that hovered over the heads of the black attorneys in this particular firm. So Richard made the most of this experience—after all, Big Southern Fried Law Firm looked impressive on his resume—and then followed his gut and moved on. (Richard was a striver.)

Let's be clear—Richard was a success. He may have faced some discrimination, bigotry, and insensitivity, but he was a success. Richard got the education he wanted, he got the job he wanted, and, most important, he got to fulfill his dream of being a litigator. You see, that's the problem that a large number of whites don't get. They truly want to believe that racism and discrimination can be avoided by a black willing and able to do the "right" things. Like growing up on the wrong side of the tracks, they want to believe that race is merely a pesky hurdle to be jumped over with the right motivation.

Well, that's not true, and I'm not going to say otherwise. Race is not an impediment, but it is a reality you work through on the road to achieving all the things you are going to achieve anyway. There aren't two groups of blacks—those who have race touch their work experience and those who don't. All blacks experience it. Some are aware of it. Some are hyperaware of it. Some have major problems with it in the workplace. Some experience only mild speed bumps in a glorious career.

But race is always a factor. Period. There is no thinking, breathing, functioning black employee who will tell you that race hasn't touched her experience if she's ever worked someplace where she was in the minority. It doesn't touch every aspect of work, but it touches enough of the overall experience to require you to empower yourself with the perspective and knowledge to make sure that your work life is as positive as you can make it. Know that when you do hit certain hurdles, you are not alone. Even if no white boss, coworker, friend, or stranger understands, I do and so do a lot of other blacks.

When it's all said and done, blacks working for whites encounter the same dilemmas, the same problems, the same concerns no matter what part of the country we live in, no matter how much or how little money we make, or how many laws, degrees, and support groups we have to protect us. We're still a potent—but small—part of the population who stand out loud and clear. With some exceptions, people have to figure out if you are Catholic, Republican, or vegetarian, but they usually don't have to figure out if you're black. Combined with the fact that

blacks are the group most associated with the civil rights movement, where you find a black person in a mostly white work environment is where you find someone who didn't get in on a free
pass. That's why when, for example, white Americans say that
they don't "see" Barack Obama's race, we all know it's bullshit.
They admire Obama so much because they know how many barriers he had to overcome, and this is why it is important for us to
work smarter before we even begin working.

How you start is how you finish.

Learn from Our Legacy

Blacks have the most complex working history of any group in
America. We don't have to travel too far up our ancestral lines to
find relatives who didn't work for pay—they worked to keep from
being beaten or killed, they worked because they and their children
(if they even got to keep them) were property, they worked because
that was the norm and they weren't supposed to remember any
other reality. This is our history. We did not try to get here by boat,
by foot, or by sneaking through any way we could to make better
lives for ourselves and our families—those are the histories of others. We were brought here as property to help others build better
lives for their own families. We were used like bricks, like horses,
like river water to provide labor for the birth of a nation.

From Middle Passage to slavery, we move to the Fifteenth
Amendment, to Jim Crow, and smack-dab up to Title VII in 1964,
which made discrimination in the workplace unlawful. Basically,
blacks did not have quite the same succession plan as other
groups. Historians have argued that with all the roadblocks put
in place, it wasn't truly until the Voting Rights Act of 1965 that

blacks actually had the right to vote. Therefore, from a practical standpoint, blacks didn't really start having the benefits of full citizenship in society until the mid-1960s. This includes the workplace.

My point is not that other ethnic groups did not have it bad, or that nonblack individuals (including whites) don't have their share of issues in the workplace. It's just that in America, the history of blacks is unique. Whatever issues our mere presence brings up with whites, they kick into place immediately. For example, in some situations the 15 percent difference gets triggered when the recruiter who takes your application puts it at the bottom of the pile because she doesn't like black people. With the exception of blacks who can pass for white (or at least nonblack), the majority of blacks do not have the option of waiting until after we prove ourselves to identify ourselves as black. It's like the old skit from the television show *In Living Color*: an overeager, too-slick brother (performed by Tommy Davidson) always has a conversation with someone that ends with him startling the person by pulling out his business card, abruptly sticking it in his or her face, and shouting "Bam!" That's what showing up at the job as a black person is like.

One of the things that I have repeatedly heard whites say is that blacks just need to "get over" slavery. It's in the past, man. Let it go, dude. They're right. Slavery is done. But the remnants of slavery continue to exist and proliferate. As black people who work, our legacy of being the descendants of bought goods still lingers. The late Johnnie Cochran was probably the single most well-known black attorney. Even with his passing, his law firm still carries his name because of his accomplishments and notoriety. We loved Thurgood Marshall and we've all heard of Clarence Thomas, but when any of us started thinking about who we would want to represent us if we were ever on trial for murder, Johnnie immediately sprang to mind. Well, did you know that Cochran's great-grandfather was a slave? Think about that for a second. Only two generations stood between Johnnie Cochran and slavery. Take that a step further. There are no slaves without slave owners. Therefore, when Cochran was going toe-to-toe with opposing counsel, witnesses, prosecutors, and judges, many of them only had two generations between them and slave owners.

This is our legacy, and we experience it every day. Less than one month before the start of 2003, Senate Majority Leader Trent Lott had to apologize for indirectly singing the praises of a segregated America. (He was later forced to resign as majority leader.) His view may not be the majority view, but it exists. In 2009 a Louisiana justice of the peace openly refused to marry interracial couples because he didn't believe in it. He felt comfortable explaining his archaic, racist, and unconstitutional reasoning right up until he stepped down from the job amid local and national pressure.

Blacks have a historical legacy of unfair treatment, but we can shape our individual legacies so that the collective goals we've achieved in this society move us forward as a people. For example, I wrote about Johnnie Cochran's situation in terms of his historical legacy, but what you had to admire about Cochran when you saw him on television was that he clearly loved what he was doing. He got a charge from being "Da Man." You can't tell me that—while I'm sure he took the O. J. Simpson trial and its aftermath very seriously—he didn't get a little kick from the fact that "If it don't fit, you must acquit" became a household phrase.

We all can't be Johnnie Cochran. But we all can aim for having work situations that empower us and make us feel that, while we may stand out, we still have infinitely more say in our work situations than our great-grandparents did.

Being Black in a New Age of Recession

I'll be the first to admit that when there was first talk of an economic downturn hitting America, I didn't believe it. I thought it was one of those scare-tactic topics that trigger a lot of news stories but thank God didn't lead to any disasters—like the Y2K fear that all computers would lock up and explode when the clock struck midnight in the year 2000, or the bird flu that will kill you the second you looked up and saw more than three birds at one time in the sky.

Unemployment for blacks in America, going back decades, has always been double the national average. That means when the nation has bad times, comparatively speaking, black folks have really bad times. That also means, statistically speaking, that the recovery for black Americans will take longer compared to the rest of the country. As hard as it is to accept or do, this requires black Americans to become more creative about how they approach their careers. Ultimately, it's always about blacks leading with their hearts to find jobs and careers that fulfill and gratify them. Sometimes, especially when times are tough economically, that's less about money than it is about furthering a dream.

After *Working While Black* was first published, my next book was *Black Out: The Black Person's Guide to Redefining a Career Path Outside of Corporate America*. I referred to and provided examples of blacks who follow the path of the Emperor (self-employment), the Artisan (pursuing a career in art), the

Hermit (being an independent contractor or a "temp"), and the Magician (leaving traditional or conventional employment for something that is neither traditional nor conventional). The point of the book is that blacks have traditionally come from the working-class ethic that says that you get a "good" job with stability, and that passion or a calling for what you do (unless called to the ministry) is irrelevant. In a nutshell, I say that passion for work has been a luxury not afforded to a culture of people who were systematically denied access to employment rights and careers until very recently. The point of *Black Out* wasn't that blacks should irresponsibly give no thought to caring for their families, paying their bills, or creating stable futures for themselves. Rather, it was to point out that responsibility and passion were not mutually exclusive.

What the recent recession should tell all of America is that since there is no job, industry, or area of the country that is recession proof, you might as well at least have a job or career that you're somewhat passionate about. There are no guarantees anyway. That's why even if your job seems pretty stable, it is still the time to explore "what if?" What if I won the lottery and never had to worry about money again? What would I do? What if I suddenly had five extra hours in the day? What would I do? Having those thoughts doesn't require you to necessarily do anything, but it may just be the kind of thinking that inspires you to take a baby step.

It's not all or nothing. The baby step might be checking out a book at the library on how to start your own business. Maybe the baby step is printing up a cheap set of business cards for the side hustle you engage in. Maybe it's finding weekend gigs to play your instrument or sing your songs. Everybody has a different dream, so everyone has a unique set of baby steps to take from where he is to where he may some day want to be. If you think and live this way, while your job or profession might not be recession proof, your mentality will be.

Therefore, for a man who loves woodworking but whose job has always been at the auto assembly plant, getting laid off could be a blessing in disguise. Yes, in the interim, the loss of money and the weight of all the things that have to be paid with money can be disabling. For some people, losing a job may legitimately be the grounds for sheer panic. But necessity is the mother of invention, and for people who have never assumed that anything about work would come easier to them in the workplace, blacks have a real opportunity to make this recession take us back to our roots.

The roots where we had our businesses in our communities. The roots where families pulled together within and with other families to build neighborhoods where everyone could thrive. The roots where black musicians and artists were respected and revered à la the Harlem Renaissance. Going back to our roots means remembering that as a culture we're rooted in resiliency.

Additionally, issues with the recession might make some go to school or back to school to get the education they've always wanted but didn't stop to get because of not wanting to walk away from the steady paycheck. Well, when the steady paycheck walks away from you, that might be the time for a "do over." A woman who loses her "good" job with the city may find that being part of the 10 percent cut from her government's department might be just the kick in the pants she needs to get financial aid and attend nursing school as she's always dreamed of doing.

You can take lemons and cry about how tart they are, or you can take the same lemons and make a slammin' lemonade. Even though it may be tougher to get a job with the recession and postrecession, and even though being black may make it that much tougher at times, you don't quit. You can't quit. You just keep trying, keep making yourself competitive, and know that in time, there will be employment or that you will find a way to employ yourself.

Learn to Be a Driver

If you're just starting off in the workforce, ask yourself what you really want to do. If you're smack-dab in the middle of the workforce, ask yourself if you want to keep doing this particular job or maintaining this career path, or if you want to do something else.

Because of our history and fear, black people tend to keep our range of choices very narrow. I know of many people who work where they work because their cousin told them a company was hiring, or because most of the people in the neighborhood work for a certain industry. In black families especially, you see that dynamic play out—you'll see a family that has four out of five children in the military or one in which all the children grew up to be middle-class professionals.

My friends know that when they seek my counsel on whether they should leave a particular job, one of my common sayings is that they should never run from a job, they should only run to a better job. In other words, don't stay in a miserable situation and then find yourself just having to get another job quickly to pay the bills. Figure out what you really want to do, then find a way to create that opportunity so that the next job begins with joy and excitement. Sometimes that great job may be something you stumble across while scanning a job-hunting search engine. But you still need to figure out who you are and what you like before you start searching.

For a black person, the ultimate strategy as a driver is to seek out the people who are most happy with their jobs and figure out how to get there. Don't go by a title. Too many people (OK, too many black people, in my opinion) judge someone's happiness by what he earns instead of asking the person whether he derives joy from what he does. We also fail to take ownership of the fact that we can be the driving force behind finding joy in whatever job we do. Sometimes moving on to the next job is not the point or the goal. Sometimes it's finding the joy in the job you have.

However, if you identify a specific new job or career you desire, be a driver—make sure you figure out exactly what stands between you and what you want. Break it down into as many small steps as you can. Think of the Chinese proverb that says, "A journey of a thousand miles begins with a single step." Maybe it's just picking up the phone and getting information from the financial aid office at your local college. Maybe it's e-mailing the company you want to work for and asking them to send you the requirements for the job listing they posted on their Web site. Part of being a successful black driver is looking inside yourself and discovering what you want instead of constantly trying to look at what decisions every other black person around you is making. So what if you're the first black to hold down a certain job? If you feel driven to do it, just assess the situation ahead of time and go for it.

The first step toward figuring out what you want to do for a living, if you haven't started yet or you want to make a change, involves getting in touch with what makes you tick. If you're forty-five and thinking about a job change, that's a lot easier than when you're eighteen and thinking about that first job. The beauty of the workforce is that you're allowed to change your mind even if the first job or the first ten jobs aren't quite right for you. Your job is not who you are, but working is what you do and should reflect who you are.

When I meet people in social settings I usually dread the part where they find out that I used to practice law, because then they superimpose a whole set of assumptions on me about my personality, my hobbies, how I grew up, and my interests. They even think they know what kind of car I must drive. (Of course, I'm embarrassed to say I sometimes do the same thing when I meet people and they tell me what they do for a living.) The truth is that most of us stumble into our jobs, careers, or professions. I didn't start law school until I was twenty-seven years old because I had never met a lawyer until I was in my midtwenties. I had always thought that people like me didn't become lawyers. I knew of only one other person in my family with a college degree, and she was a teacher, which I knew I didn't want to be.

Even as a youngster, you collect plenty of information about jobs, even if it's just figuring out what you don't want to do. If your uncle is an army major who travels around the world and you love hearing about all the places he's visited, you've got a key piece of information about yourself and what you might want to do for a living. You might not necessarily want to be in the military if you don't like regimentation, but you want a job that takes you to a lot of places. Find other jobs that provide the same opportunity to travel.

Let's say you know you are a family-oriented person. Your favorite moments involve spending time with your family. That's the most important thing to you. Knowing something as simple as that can trigger a host of questions about what kind of employment you want to have. Do you just like spending time around your own family, or do you like being around families in general?

Do you like hanging around the children or the older folks? Do you like teaching your family how to do things, or do you like being the family cook? That's an example of how the process of asking yourself questions gets you to a good answer. Exploring our maximum range of options is a skill we black Americans are still trying to teach ourselves.

One of the reasons I mentally divide blacks into the categories of survivor, striver, and thriver is because those three groups use different considerations to make decisions about where they are going to work or how they are going to make money. Think about the range of different ways there are to make money, once you eliminate those that are illegal. Some people start their own companies and businesses. Then there are the people who get degrees and enter professions. Whether professional or not, there are jobs in the private industry and jobs with the government. Within the private industry, there are small companies, medium-sized ones, and huge corporations. In addition, there are people who enlist in the military or join the Peace Corps and folks who hone their skills and talents to be entertainers or athletes. Some people find jobs that allow them to serve God, such as ministers, priests, or nuns.

This book couldn't begin to tell you enough about any of those jobs to help you make an informed decision about which one is best for you. What I am is a believer in the ability to know enough about yourself to always make a change when it is in your best interest to make the change intelligently. The book *What Color Is Your Parachute?* says that most people change jobs several times in their lifetimes. Good! As people grow, their aspirations change, just like their clothing styles or tastes in food. That's why you might have wanted to be a basketball player when you were ten years old, but when you're eighteen and about to graduate from high school, you don't really see yourself being gifted enough to have any job that involves handling a ball for pay, especially when you get more of a kick from playing with computers.

Somewhere along the line, however, people (blacks included) bought into the false belief that by eighteen or twenty-one, you were competent to make a career choice for the rest of your life. Your driver's license is still new, you just got the right to leave your mama's house without having to check in after midnight, and legally drinking in public still doesn't feel quite right, but you're supposed to pick work that you know you're going to want to do in ten, twenty, or forty years? Yeah, right.

The following are two examples of what I'm talking about— one person who doesn't sit firmly in the driver's seat and one who's not only firmly in the driver's seat but has a fastened seat belt and a road map.

First, there's a person named Georgia who keeps switching between being a survivor, a striver, and a thriver because she did not get a good hold on what exactly she wanted to do before entering the job market.

Georgia, an educated, professional black woman in her early thirties, usually cycles through the three mentalities in her job all in about a year's time. Then she moves on to another job when things don't work out. Extremely competent and with impressive credentials, Georgia gets a job and starts off as a striver, trying to beat a path of success to a higher position within her organization almost as soon as she arrives. She quickly realizes that the path to success won't be quite that direct. Once she realizes this, she becomes a thriver. Her hairdos start getting more experimental, she becomes more outspoken about controversial views, and she begins expressing a more daredevil, "what-the-f—k" attitude. The good thing is that Georgia always manages to maintain a high level of quality in her work no matter what stage she spirals in. However, at some point, either her coworkers, her boss, or her own fears start kicking in and setting off alarms. So then Georgia smooth moves to a survivor mentality, either because she's worried about keeping her job or because she gets bored enough to start looking for a new job anyplace else.

That particular cycle works for my friend Georgia, or at least until recently it has. It's worked in the past because she is incredibly gifted at each job she does, she always leaves on a good note and on her own terms, and she always lands on her feet, finding another job before she quits the one she's unhappy with.

However, what my friend is beginning to realize is that being aware of her agenda before she starts a new job is key to not defaulting from a striver into either of these other mentalities. Georgia realizes that she is getting too old not to have longevity at one job in a career that respects staying power. Since at her essence Georgia is a striver, being a survivor or a thriver are fallback mechanisms for her. She needs to figure out what she ultimately wants to do and find a job that gets her there from day one.

In Georgia's defense, it wasn't exactly that she hadn't thought about what she wanted to do. She had thought about it. How-

ever, like a lot of first-generation college students in black families, she didn't have any role models for how to figure out a life
path. She picked philosophy as her undergraduate major but then
felt she needed to go to graduate school to get a practical job.
However, once she got the practical graduate degree, she spent
the next few years job-hopping in frustration.

The second example—of someone who has undertaken his
career as a driver and been successful—is a brother I know who
scoped out his life goals and career plan from the beginning.

> Tony came from a background where he wasn't the first gen-
> eration to go to college, own a business, or earn middle-class
> pocket change. Since Tony knew he wanted to be in politics
> by thirty years of age, when it came time to pick one of two
> companies who offered him a job right out of college, he
> picked the company that had the better track record where
> blacks were concerned. Ironically, the company he rejected
> had more blacks working there, but those blacks encoun-
> tered more obstacles and were more crowded around the
> bottom of the ladder. Tony was the prototype of a black
> striver, and he wasn't about to slow his path to the pinnacle.
> Tony ran for city council at the age of thirty but missed win-
> ning the election by a hair—and he ran against an estab-
> lished white incumbent. There's no doubt in my mind that
> with the name recognition he acquired, the community sup-
> port he built, and the taste of victory in his well-honed taste
> buds, Tony will only be off by a couple of years in meeting
> his goal of holding political office.

My point isn't that Tony is Mr. Golden Black Man who made perfect decisions and encountered no roadblocks in his career path. It certainly is not to imply that his path didn't come littered with those same 15 percent issues that Georgia's did. It's just that because his plan was so fixed in his mind and his path was so sure, those 15 percent issues were obstacles he got around differently. He wasn't luckier or smarter than Georgia. His people just had a head start on Georgia's people in whittling out better opportunities and success strategies that were then passed down to Tony.

Figure Out Where and How to Work

I can't tell you how to pick a job or a career. That's part of the 85 percent everyone has to figure out for him- or herself. But some ways to help you figure out where to work and how to work include

- using your favorite job search engine such as CareerBuilder.com or Indeed.com to see what jobs are available in your area and, starting with the first one, writing down any and all that interest you, regardless of your qualifications;
- talking to people about what they do and do not like about their jobs;
- going to the library and checking out the career section;
- seeking out a headhunter or a job coach; and
- exposing yourself to as many different kinds of jobs and careers as you can to see what fits.

My personal philosophy, as I've gotten older and a little further along in my own career, is that I don't look for jobs, I create opportunities. Rather than looking for a job and then figuring out whether I want to do that particular set of duties, I find I'm happier when I figure out what I like to do and find the opportunity that pays me to do it. I wish I had approached jobs that way when I started my career, because it would have saved me at least a couple of wrong turns. Of course, the truth is, the wrong turns taught me lessons each time that helped with the next round of decisions.

Even a black person right out of high school or college can create opportunities if she does her homework and thinks carefully about what she wants. What's your intention? Are you looking for a job or a career? A trade or a profession? If you don't know, you may end up someplace you don't like. It's like the old joke about the person who got lost while driving but made good time getting to the place where he ended up. When it comes to working, you should never stop asking yourself these questions unless you're deliriously happy with what you're doing. In fact, the longer you ask these questions without paying attention to your own answers, the longer it takes you to find the right vocation for you.

A friend of mine is a beautiful and brilliant sister in her early thirties who wants to be a doctor. She has wanted to be a doctor for years and keeps going back to college for classes and the occasional degree or certification. She also finds jobs in the health care industry, which is the equivalent of having her nose pressed against a store window. I once asked her why, since she's single and has no kids, she just didn't go to medical school full-time. Her answer was that by the time she took the necessary courses, studied, took the MCAT, graduated from medical school, and did a residency or two, she would be in her forties. Of course, I made the classic response by asking her if she wasn't going to be in her forties in seven or eight years anyway. One day I think she'll go to medical school and kick herself for not starting earlier. Or she won't and will spend her forties and the years after regretting not having done so.

Another friend of mine waited until her midforties to get a college degree. She did this after raising a family, divorcing a husband, and working more than a dozen years at a utility company. After she achieved this first degree, she got the itch and kept going to school until she ended up with a PhD and now, in her sixties, is a college professor. She focused on a dream and her intention, asked the right questions of herself and others, did the research, dug for the resources, and ended up doing what she wanted to do. So what if she started this career in her fifties? She was happy every step of the way. Did she ever and does she still face discrimination in a world that kneels at the altars of youth, fair skin, and masculinity? Yes, of course. But because she knew what she wanted, she surrounded herself with the energy, the information, and the people who helped her navigate those waters.

Not everyone aims to be a doctor or a college professor. It may be that your goal is to get an earlier work shift so that you can spend more time with your kids or to be a disc jockey at a radio station rather than just listening to the radio while you input computer data. The point is that picking a job or a career is not something you do once in your life. Examining whether you are happy and fulfilled in what you do for pay is an ongoing journey with no real destination until you stop working.

Again, the point is not that you get around the 15 percent issues of being black in the workplace by picking the "right" job or career; rather, it is that you withstand those 15 percent issues better when you pick the job or career that is right for you.

3

AIN'T TOO PROUD TO BEG

How Blacks Get Through
the Door in the First Place

■

Maggie was the first person in her family to go to college. She was raised by a single mother, and Maggie had three children herself by the age of eighteen.

By the time Maggie graduated from college, she was a striver pure and simple, ready to take on the world and make a better life for herself and her children. When she was about to graduate from engineering school, she was, therefore, quite proud of her accomplishments. She felt like it reflected well on her character and tenacity that she could graduate from college while raising children. In the accomplishments section of her resume, Maggie always listed raising her children,

including each of their ages. She wondered why she had trouble getting called back for job interviews.

Maggie had every right to be proud of her achievements as a
black woman raising three children with little help from either
the fathers of the children or her own family, but we live in a
world of stereotypes. In addition to listing her three children and
their ages, Maggie also gave a detailed list of the black associa-
tions she belonged to, such as the college chapter of the NAACP
and the black engineering students' organization. Therefore, anyone simply skimming her resume saw the neon light flashing "single black mother up ahead." Even for a thriver, a black employee
who lives life according to his or her own rhythm, that's too much
information before you get to the interview stage.

Is the point that Maggie was supposed to hide the fact that
she had children? No, because the information itself was not the
issue. What Maggie needed to do was keep in mind the 15 percent factor. When applying for a job, any mother, regardless of
race, must be particularly wise regarding the appropriate time to
reveal this information. A black single mother needs to be particularly sensitive. The bottom line is that there is a stereotype
that black women and girls are more promiscuous than white
women and girls. Therefore, Maggie should have anticipated that,
employment laws aside, future employers might jump to the conclusion that she had some wild streak as a teenager—one she still
might have as an adult. Leaving the information about her children off her resume will buy Maggie the necessary window of
time to impress a potential employer with her qualifications. In

doing this, she doesn't give them a chance to jump to conclusions just from looking at a piece of paper.

Jeremy is a journalist who applies for jobs in his profession carefully, strategically, and with audacity. Since college he has been clear about what he wants to do with his career and his life. His goals included working at his hometown newspaper, then working at well-respected national newspapers, and ultimately winning prestigious awards for his writing. By age forty, Jeremy had done all three. He wasn't merely responding to life, he had made himself the driving force deciding the path of his professional life.

One of the ways he did this was by learning from his mistakes—or figuring out why his actions didn't always match the results he wanted. For example, early on in his career when he applied for jobs he didn't get, sometimes he would politely ask an interviewer what he could have done differently to get the job. He adjusted (never falsified) his resume when necessary, changed his interview style when suggested, and used his results (plus further investigation) as his learning tools. For example, when one potential employer told Jeremy that he needed more hard news experience to supplement his extensive feature writing experience, he made a point of asking for more opportunities to cover breaking news stories at the newspaper where he worked (without telling his current employer why) before applying for other jobs.

In terms of applying for a job, Jeremy is clearly a driver. While instinctively a striver, Jeremy becomes a driver when he takes his strategy one step further. While the striver operates from ambition, a driver operates from the best instincts of the survivor (such as to not do anything that endangers getting or keeping a job) and the thriver (such as operating with his own flair), while keeping the liabilities of those modes to a minimum.

Jeremy recognized that when it comes to getting a job, he pays more attention to the 85 percent issues—how he as a potential employee is well suited for a particular job—in order to eliminate any doubts that this potential employee, who happens to be black, can do the job and do it well.

How can Maggie be a driver? By realizing that, ultimately, no employer really cares whether you have a kid or not as long as having children won't interfere with how you perform your job. Therefore, Maggie should highlight the qualifications that make her stand out as the best person for a particular job. This needs to be her driving motivation. That's where research, like what Jeremy did, comes in handy. If you've done basic research to figure out what skills you need to excel in a particular corporate culture and what the job qualifications are for a particular position, then it's not a stretch to list the qualifications you have that make you stand out as a strong candidate for the job.

This chapter deals with one of the first ways that the 15 percent issue can rear its head for a black employee. After all, if race is going to be an issue in the workplace, getting through the door is probably the first place it will come up. For example, a study in 2002 conducted by two professors from the Massachusetts Institute of Technology and the University of Chicago Graduate School of Business found that resumes with black-sounding names got half as many responses from employers as resumes from those with race-neutral names.

What Am I Looking for, Anyway?

The question is, what information is a black person supposed to be fishing for when figuring out how to get through the door? A black person who is a survivor will be the type of person who needs the least amount of information. Ultimately, his work experience is not going to be affected one way or the other. As long as there is not a huge discrepancy between what he makes and what others doing the same job make, he will be fine with the money issue. Survivors care somewhat if other blacks work with them, but usually it will not be a deal breaker.

Strivers, on the other hand, will need to know a lot of—pardon the pun—black-and-white information. How many blacks work at the company? What positions do they hold? What prompted the blacks who left to leave? Has a black person ever done the job I'm hired to do? Has a black ever been promoted to the types of jobs I might want to do?

Thrivers have the toughest research job of all, because their research will center on style and culture and the intangible things that can determine whether they despise going to work. Is it corporate clingy or laid-back smooth? Is the place weighed down with rules and regulations? Will I get fired for expressing opinions? Am I going to stand out to the point where it will interfere with me doing my job? A thriver finds this out by asking about the personalities of the black folks and the white folks. More important, the thriver finds this out by figuring out what blacks work there and why. A thriver may or may not be what the employer thinks of as a troublemaker, but you definitely don't want to walk into an environment where you will almost certainly be labeled one because of how you compare to everyone else.

On the surface, it's all an 85 percent issue. Employers advertise for jobs, "equal employment opportunity" signs are hung all over, and affirmative action programs still exist. It doesn't seem like it should be that complicated. However, statistics show that the two areas of life where blacks probably experience the most discrimination are in employment and housing. According to a review of the latest U.S. Census data, a black household made an average of $649 for every $1,000 that a white household made. There aren't any statistics that show how many blacks are turned away at the hiring stage because of race, since no employer is going to admit to that reason in a survey and every employee who believes race is the reason doesn't necessarily report it. But with such a huge disparity between white and black incomes, it's clear that more higher paying jobs are going to whites than to blacks.

Going After the Job You Want

You should never apply for a job unless you know you want it. A black person has to go through an extra analysis of how race may play a role in a workplace that may be predominantly white. Taking the time to do this extra analysis thoroughly is never more important than before you interview to get a job. Whether you are a survivor, a striver, or a thriver makes no difference if you don't get the job in the first place or if you get the wrong job.

Usually, getting a job with anyone, particularly a white employer, starts off with that first piece of paper. For some blacks, that first piece of paper is a job application; for others it's a resume. Sometimes it's both. Sometimes it's just seeing an ad and showing up. But at some point, you are expected to put in print things about yourself that reveal who you are and tell your employer who you're going to be as a worker. So be sure you want the job—any job—before you go through all the trouble to do your extra evaluation and research.

Research, Research, Research

One of the first things that a black person needs to do before applying for a job is research the company. It's amazing to me how few people do that. As far as I'm concerned, it's an essential step to decide if you even want to work for a given company. Even if your research comes up empty or you get wrong information, it's far better than the alternative—trying to drive at night with your headlights off.

For blacks, getting the lowdown on a company is critical information. You've got to know how many other blacks work there, how many of them are managers or supervisors, and what the story is about the blacks who no longer work there. Being a former newspaper reporter, I'm usually the go-to guy for my friends when they want advice on how to find out this kind of information. My standard reply is that they start with common sense and move on from there.

The great little secret about being black is that what whites suspect is true—we truly do all know each other. OK, maybe we don't directly, but there usually is an indirect line from you to a black person who knows something about Corporation X. Ask

your mama. Ask your cousin Peaches. Ask another black person
in the industry. Pick the brains of your white friends. If you
choose your white friends with as much care as I do, then they
will be almost as likely as most blacks to give you the lowdown
on what the environment is really like. When you don't take
advantage of the six degrees of separation that exist between you
and your next job, you're playing Negro Roulette if you take the
job.

> Malika went to work for a marketing company. She had heard
> good things about the company in general, so she focused
> on the overall reputation of the organization within the
> industry and figured any other issues wouldn't be important.
> Well, she got the job, and even though it was the year 2000,
> she found herself the first black ever hired by the company
> and the only woman to be hired in a management position.
> That by itself would not have been a problem, except for the
> fact that nobody in the company but the pseudoliberal who
> hired Malika was particularly interested in having a black
> woman working there, especially a black woman who made
> more money than just about everyone else in the company.

With just a little research and attention to the red flags,
Malika might have saved herself the trouble of being an experi-
ment that failed in a company that drained her spirit, zapped her
confidence, and converted her from being a thriver to a survivor
when she got her next job. Malika endured constant exclusion

from lunch and other social activities (which furthered her political isolation within the company), repeated criticism about her lack of experience in a certain area of marketing (which she told them up front that she didn't have), and numerous comments about her salary and "how well" she was being paid compared to others.

Again, a good decision hinges on good research, and good research depends on knowing what you want before you have to make a decision. It's imperative that you choose job situations that put you where you want to be based on your individual goals. Identifying those goals first will help make your research more directed and efficient.

Job Applications and Resumes

People who apply for jobs by filling out job applications, in some ways, have it easy. The person taking your application can see that you are black. You won't have the initial problem of an interviewer being caught off guard, in the event that your being black is going to catch someone by surprise. Although the person who collects the applications may not be the person who actually interviews, I always assume that information about your race gets passed along if it's not the majority. It's sort of like when you read a novel and the writer never mentions when the character is white but always makes a point of mentioning if the person is black or Hispanic or Asian.

Resumes pose a trickier problem. Asking yourself important questions as you create your resume can't be avoided. Should I or shouldn't I put something down that indicates I'm black? Or should I play the *Guess Who's Coming to Dinner* surprise move and let them find out when I show up? In December 2009, a column in the *New York Times* headlined "Whitening the Resume" addressed how in a bad economy, black job applicants had to give even more attention than ever to thinking about the ways their resume could be tweaked to avoid indicating their race, since blacks were having a harder time than whites in getting called for job interviews.

Again, how you start is how you finish. That's why sitting down and asking yourself what your mode of operation is will answer that question for you. Some people, for example, want prospective employers to know up front that they are black so that a problem can be knocked out early. That has always been my personal philosophy, but even that may not be a clear-cut decision.

Are you essentially a survivor? Do you just want a job where you put in your time, collect your paycheck, and ease on down that road to retirement, or at least to steady paychecks until a better gig comes along? Then leave off all references to being black. Don't mention groups or organizations that have the word *black* in the title. That gets you two things. One, if they don't know you're black before you come in for the interview, many white employers will either not care that you are black or will be pleasantly surprised that you didn't broadcast it before the interview. Two, for the segment of employers who are supersensitive about race issues, an employer will be too focused on the reasons why she should hire you if she likes your resume than on worrying about the ways you may or may not fit into the organization once you get hired. Your personal employment goals will dictate how you react.

A striver wants to get through the door to get ahead. Therefore, a striver will be more concerned with the total package than whether or not he makes too many references to his race. The striver's resume will wave flags like "Professional Society of Black Engineers," "Black Secretaries of America," "Human Resources Black America." That's not a bad idea if done with a light hand. It portrays the applicant as being serious about his or her career without necessarily coming off as "militant."

Now the thriver just ain't going to care. If she is the media spokesperson for her hometown chapter of the Black Panthers, that's going to have a high spot on her resume. The thriver will not be ashamed to tell you in bold letters on her resume that she was one of the founding chapter members of the All Black Symphony in her hometown. No accomplishment is off-limits for a thriver. Accomplishments, awards, and accolades that relate directly to black people are exactly what the thriver will highlight, if that is important to her.

The point is not that thrivers are going to be the biggest problack folks in the workplace. It's just that white people will think they will be. (On a personal note: I've never understood why most whites confuse exuberance, loudness, or even passion with militancy. Many a time I've been the person that my white supervisors just knew "wanted to be starting sumthin'," but a good two-thirds of the time, it was my nice, quiet, low-to-the-ground brother or sister who stood ready to riot and storm the gates when a problem arose.)

Guess Who's Coming to the Interview

One thing to remember as a black person trying to get that foot through the door, whether you're right out of school or you're working on your tenth job since the 1970s, is that who you are on paper is not necessarily who they are going to get as an employee.

You're trying to get a job, not bare your soul. Keeping anything other than need-to-know information off a resume or job application is not lying. (Warning: Never, ever, ever lie on a resume. As a reporter, I've seen careers ruined with a lie; as an attorney, I've seen lawsuits crumble over one lie.)

Beth provides a fine example of a resume that just screams blonde-haired, blue-eyed preppie: Ivy League school, cultured last name, corporate specializations, and classy hobbies and memberships, including a membership in the National Bar Association. Oops. The NBA (also known as the other NBA) is *also* known as "the black lawyers group." Well, what you see is what you get.

More than once, Beth has seen the look on the faces of interviewers change to blatant surprise when the porcelain-pale maiden they expected turned out to be a dark shade of mahogany. Some jobs she didn't get. Some she did. But Beth's interviewers almost always got a surprise.

Affirmative Action or Acting

In the United States, one of the most interesting phenomena to me is that people think blacks are getting jobs left and right because of affirmative action. You know who I hear that from the most? Whites who didn't get jobs they wanted. Even if they don't know the race of the person who got the job, they'll swear on their own personal Bibles that they didn't get the job because of affirmative action.

What black folks know is that if affirmative action even crosses the mind of someone who is hiring us, that's not a good thing, because it means we will be held up to some artificial black standard we'll never live up to. For years, I've called it the "Super Nig" mentality. The Super Nig is supposed to do an A-plus job at all times, make no mistakes, and have hobbies and interests that make them fit in with all the white folks so that the company can pat itself on the back for finding such an "articulate" and "extraordinary" black hire. When ordinary black folks can't live up to the artificial perfection expected of Super Nig, that affirmative-action-thinking employer feels justified in raising the standards even higher for the next black hire. My point isn't that every employer or supervisor harbors this mentality, but it is more prevalent than whites want to admit. It is the tendency to view the imperfections of black employees with a little more harshness if the workplace has very few blacks. Part of that comes from the fact that many whites are only used to dealing with blacks in forced environments—school and work—so stereotypes, usually dealing with work ethic or intelligence, do get passed on. Pretty much all black people are fighting a stereotype unless they work in the type of job where many blacks have come before them.

Frank was a white reporter I used to work with who got passed over for about four different beat assignments in the two years I worked with him. Every time he didn't get the request, he would loudly say (in a room filled with black and Hispanic reporters) that affirmative action was the reason he couldn't get ahead.

I really wanted to be the one to tell him how it was the original affirmative action—for white males—that got his incompetent ass hired in the first place and kept him from being fired in the second place, but I never wanted to put myself on the line by saying it.

In all the hundreds of employment cases I've been involved with as an attorney, I've never heard an employer use affirmative action or quotas as the reason for hiring a particular person of color, as opposed to having a general affirmative action plan. Actually, it tends to be the opposite. When white employers want to fire a black person (or a member of another ethnic group), fear of being accused of discrimination is what keeps them from firing the person sooner rather than later, even when it is a pretty clear-cut case. An example is when a company let a black male manager stay on for an indefinite period of time, even after the company had received reliable written statements from his female subordinates accusing him of sexual harassment. The company was more afraid of a race discrimination claim from the black manager than of the sexual harassment claims from the female employees. Believe it or not, that hesitancy happens more than black folks think.

Ultimately, getting caught up in a company's affirmative action plan (or lack of one) doesn't do the average black person any good. Some of the best, fairest companies to work for don't have a formal plan at all, while some of the most racist, bigoted companies will occasionally pay an advertising company to tout them as the place to be if you're a person of color. That is why cultivating good instincts is one of the most valuable tools any person, but particularly a black person, can cultivate in the job-hunting game. You have to fine-tune your ability to gauge whether someone in the interviewing process doesn't care for you regardless of your race or whether the company or the department has general problems with hiring blacks. How do you cultivate those instincts? By listening carefully, taking good mental notes, paying attention to your physical reactions, and then evaluating the outcome.

Lawful Questioning Only, Please

Under the law there are certain kinds of questions that potential employers cannot ask you. But just because employers can't ask the questions does not mean that they can't read between the lines and blow you off anyway. Since getting the job is your goal, however, it may be in your best interest to address the underlying concern that even an unlawful question asks.

For example, a potential employer can usually ask you about criminal convictions relating to traffic violations and, in general, about criminal problems that relate directly to the job you are applying for. For example, if you're applying for a job to be a long-haul driver, your new boss has the right to know about those five speeding tickets you've received in the past seven years, because there is a direct correlation between your illegal speeding and what the potential employer is hiring you to do. Employers have legal liability for the employees they hire, so they have the right and the duty to ask. Similarly, if you apply for a job as a bookkeeper, your potential boss can ask you if you have any criminal convictions relating to whether you have a tendency to poach money. Again, the company has a duty to ask because they can get sued for negligent hiring otherwise.

Employers are not supposed to ask job applicants about arrests, however. The U.S. Department of Labor has recognized that asking about arrests is a loaded and particularly discriminatory question since (1) an arrest is no indication of guilt, and

(2) minorities have historically suffered (and still suffer) more arrests than whites.

Credit is another tough one. Unless there is a business necessity (such as in any job at a bank that involves the handling of other people's money), the U.S. Department of Labor has determined that, in general, potential employees should not be asked about their credit records, because those records tend to have an adverse effect on minorities. You need to read carefully any general waivers you sign when you apply for a job, however, because you may be signing a release that allows an employer to get a copy of your credit report. (The issue of credit is a book-length subject, but know that, traditionally, blacks have less money and worse credit than whites for reasons ranging from access to education to racism. Therefore, working to achieve and maintain good credit might end up being as important a factor in getting a job as in getting a new car.)

Kevin is a black man with a master's degree who lived overseas as a business consultant. He wanted to come back to America to be closer to his family. Actually, he didn't want to be too close to his Indiana-based family, but close enough in case of an emergency. He applied for the perfect job in Atlanta. In his interview, Kevin signed a waiver allowing the company, a national corporation, to look at his credit report, his criminal records, any open civil records (such as being a party in a lawsuit), and basically everything else that could be uncovered about him with nothing more than a Social Security number. On the condition that everything from the background check turned out fine, the Atlanta company made a conditional job offer to Kevin. Kevin was confident that everything would work out just fine, so he quit his then-current job, packed his bags, and found an apartment in Atlanta. While visiting his family in Indiana, waiting to start his new life, Kevin received word from the Atlanta firm that the job offer was rescinded based on a troubling credit report.

That's the nature of the at-will employment thing. (*At-will employment* means you can quit without giving a reason, and, with the exception of illegal discrimination or an employment contract, a company can fire you without giving a reason.) Kevin had no employment contract, the company made sure the offer was conditional to cover themselves, and Kevin had given the company written permission to do this investigation.

Unfair? Maybe. Unlawful? Not necessarily.

Kevin could have avoided this circumstance by not quitting the job he had until the background check was officially over and the new company made a firm offer, but what he went through is an important lesson to learn whether you're a survivor, striver, or thriver. First, don't be a sitting duck. Before you start job searching, do your research to see if you're in an industry that requires background checks. If you are, or if you suspect there may be a problem with your credit, your criminal background, or an outstanding lawsuit against you, attempt to resolve the problems before you start job hunting.

Alternatively, you can prepare a preemptive strike. If you are asked to sign a waiver for purposes of a background check, you might want to offer up anything that could be a potential problem before you actually sign the paper. Sometimes the very act of revealing it yourself and explaining your own concern about the impression it makes may be enough to keep the information from being a problem for the employer.

The problem with a preemptive strike is that you might alert a potential employer to an issue that they might never red flag independently. Truth is, just because a company says they will do a background check doesn't mean they really will or that they'll closely examine what they find. The key thing is to anticipate the potential problem in your background and be prepared with a contextual explanation about how the situation arose. For example, you were going through a divorce at the time your credit went sour, or the DUI came the night of your baby sister's college graduation. Don't lie, just be prepared to do damage control. Most important, when the new employer says the job is conditional or in any way implies the background check is still ongoing, don't make a move—literally or figuratively—until you have an actual offer.

A woman named Olivia, who had a handful of cute kids, applied for a job as a paralegal. Olivia mentioned her children during the interview. Olivia got the job. The main attorney responsible for hiring Olivia patted herself on the back to several people about how she gave a poor, black, single mother a job. She was proud of her contribution to society. The only little problem was that Olivia had a husband—a great, hardworking, upstanding brother. That kind of blew the mind of the old girl attempting to help the black race uplift itself. Suddenly, Olivia was Public Enemy Number One—she couldn't get a break from the partner who previously was her biggest supporter. Stereotypes are a bitch, ain't they?

So what's the solution? Maggie mentions her kids on her resume and can't get a break; Olivia mentions her kids in the interview and gets too much of one. Children are really beside the point. Maggie's problem was one she could have anticipated and warded off with artful timing. Olivia just had the misfortune of applying for a job with an interviewer who had issues. Sometimes the employer can reveal those problematic issues as early as the interview stage.

Interviewing is the first dance you have with your potential employers. They can ask good questions, which allow you to convince them to offer you a job, or they can ask really bad questions that leave you in a trick bag. Some of those bad questions can be downright unlawful. Knowing the difference will help you navigate these potentially treacherous waters.

What happens when someone is asked an unlawful question during a job interview? For example, a woman who is asked if her husband will mind the long hours she has to work (assuming that the candidate has volunteered that she is married, because asking is typically unlawful) might choose to answer the question because she is burning to have that particular job. But because it is unlawful, there are other ways she could handle it. She could directly confront the person who asked the question by pointing out that it is unlawful. But then she risks being perceived as defensive. However, if she were indifferent about getting the job, she could report it to her state human rights office or the federal Equal Employment Opportunity Commission.

The key thing to remember when interviewing is to keep your eye on the prize; in other words, focus on getting the job offer in the first place before you decide whether you want to accept it. If you're concerned with getting the job, it may not be the best strategy for you to be thinking simultaneously about whether a question is illegal or not. Be more concerned with what the questions you are being asked reveal to you about your fit with that job or that supervisor. Take note of what topics the interviewer appears to keep getting back to. Is he concerned about your extracurricular activities? Does he keep dancing around the topic of any possible family distractions? Does he seem to focus on aspects of the job that you don't have a lot of experience and/or interest in? Take the questions asked as information to file away for your own decision-making process. That will help you determine your fit into that company or office.

Another preemployment matter that can come up is job testing. Some careers and jobs require them. How do you handle them? That's a tough one, because a variety of tests exists. There are civil service exams, which you can study for. Then there are personality tests, which you can't study for because, well, they're supposed to reveal your personality.

Many standardized tests have been criticized for reflecting cultural bias. They're written by white people to hire white people. No universal tips exist for taking any of them except for the obvious, such as asking if there are study aids or classes and taking advantage of them. If you know that a test will be given, take the time to study for it. If you really want the job, it won't feel like a burden. Give yourself every opportunity to succeed and don't assume cultural bias. Remember that unless your prospective employer is singling you out to take a test, which you could only learn about by talking to others applying for the same job, just chalk that up to the price that everyone has to pay to get the job. As long as you are confident that everyone applying for the job takes the test, you know you have an 85 percent issue.

How will you know when the 15 percent factor kicks in? You really won't unless you didn't get the job based on the tests and you challenge the company.

Adjusting Your Strategy in Hard Economic Times

When the economy goes belly up, sometimes the trick is getting any job. And since blacks historically have twice the unemployment rate as whites in this country, hard economic times hit blacks doubly hard. Therefore, sometimes the dream job just has to wait. When circumstances place you in the position of needing to find a job quickly for survival's sake, how do you speed up the process? First, you have to investigate who is hiring. In part, you can look through the Sunday want ads and online job sites to see who has available positions. If you're a professional, then you can ask colleagues to recommend a good headhunter. (A headhunter puts professionals looking for jobs in touch with employers.) Employment agencies do the same thing for job hunters. Sometimes a middleman can speed up the process of looking for a job, but it will rarely be a good idea to rely on just that avenue. Working for a temporary agency might also be another way to get an idea of what's going on in a particular industry—a chance to get your feet wet before you dive in.

As far as taking advantage of affirmative action—good luck. Companies usually don't advertise or publicize their affirmative action goals for purposes of hiring. You might hear about them by word of mouth, but the signs advertising "Equal Opportunity Employer" are the equivalent of a restaurant with a sign that says "Our Kitchen Passes the Health Code."

Unfortunately, figuring out whether you've been discriminated against at the hiring stage is difficult to determine because you don't have a personal track record with the company. In other words, a rejection is usually a terse, impersonal communication without an explanation.

Some Final Thoughts

If you're experiencing an ongoing problem with finding a job, the problem may be with your job references. One of the ways you can test what your former employers are saying about you is to convince an intelligent-sounding and trustworthy friend to pretend to be a potential employer who is checking references you listed on your resume or application. It may be that you've been blackballed by getting negative references from one or more of your former employers. While some states allow you to sue your former employer for giving a bad reference (which is why many employers give out almost no real information anymore when another company calls for a reference), your real priority needs to be getting a job ASAP. A bad reference or just a plain uninspiring one will require you to think about providing another name or obtaining a written letter of reference that overflows with accolades.

Also, in job hunting, following up with a thank-you note to the interviewers is always a good idea. I've actually heard interviewers say the person who sent the note got the edge over all the other equally qualified candidates who didn't. That is an example of having the 15 percent difference work in your favor. To the extent that an interviewer has bad impressions about blacks, even showing politeness and courtesy will make you stand out in a positive way, which might help counteract a stereotype.

How you start is how you finish. So, in clarifying your intention before you begin job hunting, you have a much better likelihood of getting the job or career in the industry you want.

4

TALKING GOOD AND WELL

■

Martin had worked at his job as a manager of a Dallas department store for six months. He received his MBA from the
same black university where he'd received his undergraduate degree, which means he had minimal experience being
around whites before this job.

He thought things were going well, but he wasn't quite
sure. Martin figured that now, after being there for half a
year, it was time to get some feedback from his boss, Jack.
"So, Jack, I'm thinking of buying a brand-new car. Before I
do that, I was curious about what you thought of my work
performance." Jack heartily responded, talking about the joy
and excitement of buying a brand-new car. He encouraged
Martin to run out and buy one. However, Jack did not
address the question about Martin's work performance. Mar-

tin assumed, however, that Jack was impying that he was doing a good job and that he had enough job security to make a major purchase. After all, Martin reasoned, he wouldn't put someone in that situation.

Based on his conversation with Jack, Martin got his first new car that weekend, complete with his first car payment. Two weeks later, Jack gave Martin his evaluation and his two weeks' notice, stating that his job was terminated due to extensive performance problems that dated back to when Martin first started.

Effective communication is probably one of the most important skills for success in the workplace. That's one of those 85 percent issues, relevant to every employee, since everyone needs good communication skills to get along and get ahead. For a black employee, however, good communication is critical. When it is not done in a style compatible with the place a person works, an employee can easily find him- or herself dealing with that 15 percent difference.

What does it mean to communicate well? It is communication that gets your point across to the listener exactly as you intend; that is, the listener gets the point you are trying to make. Good communication covers both the written and the spoken word. Good communication also includes the subtle body language that either deflects or reinforces what you are trying to say.

In the example above, Martin may have thought he was communicating well, but he wasn't. If he had been paying attention to Jack all along, he would have observed that Jack was not a very direct person. He would have observed this from the way Jack dealt with other people, saying one thing to people in Martin's presence and then saying what he really thought after they left. It was not that Jack was dishonest; Jack was just less than direct.

One of the biggest culture shocks for blacks who do not have any significant contact with whites until they are grown or nearly grown is dealing with the white tendency to be less direct than what most of us are used to.

Martin's boss, Jack, knew that he was about to terminate Martin when Martin asked about buying the car, because the performance problems dated back to the time when Martin started. But Jack felt he was being polite. In terms of communication, whites are more indirect and more concerned about politeness, unless the words are cloaked in authority. The direct thing for Jack to have said was, "Martin, if I were you, I wouldn't even buy a scooter until after you've had your evaluation."

Let's face it, with a few Cosby-type exceptions, black folks on the home front are vocal and direct. Even when the voice isn't loud, it's strong. Most blacks—from twenty to sixty—did not grow up in a household of "time-outs" and "sit in the corner." Most of us grew up in households where if there were not outright ass whuppings, there were plenty of threats of them. The words we grew up hearing were along the lines of: "No, 'cuz I said so." "I brought you into this world—I can take you out." "You bet not." "Do what I said to do, not what you see me do." "Boy, if you do that one more time." "Girl, if you don't stop that right this minute." "Nunya—that stands for none of your business."

Clear. Simple. Direct. No room for ambiguity. Tons of drama, but plenty of clarity. When you broke a rule, you knew you were breaking one, and you knew there would be plenty to say on someone's part (not yours) if you got caught. No, not all black people grew up that way. And yes, some folks who aren't black grow up that way.

Indirect Directness

In general, direct communication, even in very imperfect, dysfunctional households, is something that more black people are familiar with than probably any other group of people. That's why the more understated, if not downright passive-aggressive, forms of communication that many whites engage in can create absolute culture shock when blacks enter a work world populated by whites.

I've always informally made this observation as an employee. As an attorney, I've seen how black folks can have even more of a tendency to increase their directness and come off as confrontational when they encounter problems at work. In general, long before it gets to an employee filing a complaint or a lawsuit, a black employee doesn't deal with bad news with soft energy. Even when negative information is not being conveyed during everyday conversation, the black style of communication can be rattling to whites who are not used to it.

Because I am extremely direct, probably even more so than the average black person, my style requires a bit of acclimation for the whites who work with me. In many places I have worked, most of the whites actually find it a refreshing change of pace, but my challenge (one I still struggle with) is learning when to curb my directness so that what I'm trying to say doesn't get lost in the style in which I say it.

I was happy to see that a study on cultural communication (Toolkit for Cross-Cultural Collaboration, 1999) emphasized what I had always observed about the ways different racial groups communicate. This study compared the different communication styles of blacks, whites, Native Americans, Asians, and Hispanics. Among the findings were that:

- Blacks communicate with much more animation and emotional expression than any other group.
- Blacks and Hispanics communicate with more gestures than other groups.
- Blacks speak with somewhat more volume than any other group. (To put it in my own words, energetically, we black people take up a lot of space.)

A driver brings his or her style of communication to the workplace with both the intention to speak and the intention to be heard. A driver knows that every time you open your mouth at work or put words to paper or a computer screen, you drive either closer to your goals or further away from them.

In a company where no one but white males ran things, Jewel, a stylish and focused sister in her late twenties, had the executives regularly eating out of her French-manicured hands. Jewel got that a woman didn't need to sleep her way to the top; she just had to listen her way to the top. She listened carefully to how each executive spoke to her about job assignments, and when she spoke back, she mirrored his language and tempo and listened for the hidden nuances of what he didn't say. For example, when dealing with the fidgety, high-tempo supervisors, Jewel spoke quickly and to the point. However, when dealing with the slower, more laid-back higher-ups, Jewel's cadence would be more like molasses, slow and sweet. Jewel had found that when you learn to match your pace to that of your speakers, they feel more comfortable with you, thus telling you more about how to meet their work needs.

Jewel is a driver whose communication style usually gets her exactly what she wants. Instead of doing one-size-fits-all work for each honcho, Jewel tailors her approach and her results to each person to maximize her relationship with each executive. Because Jewel listened well and mirrored—not mimicked—their styles of communication, she received their trust, and they looked at her work with the expectation that it would provide what they required and more.

Where Jewel's particular gift lay was in recognizing that as a young, attractive black woman in Corporate America, she had to get right to the 85 percent similarity and dwell in that 15 percent difference zone no longer than she had to. Getting great credentials in the first place got her to the starting line, but talking her employers' language helped drive her to a winning finish.

Sounding White, Talking Black

In January 2010, it was reported that during the campaign of Barack Obama, Senate Majority Leader Harry Reid said that he believed a black man had a chance of winning the presidency, especially one who spoke with "no Negro dialect, unless he wanted to have one." Statements like that, unfortunately, reinforce the perception that speaking well means speaking white.

We live in a society where we all know what the phrase "sounds black" means when describing how someone speaks. If you're an educated black person who sounds as if you went to a predominantly white private or suburban public school while growing up, you know the sting of having another black person tell you that you "talk white."

Language is the most important way we define and describe ourselves, once we get past race and gender. Language, however, isn't just about words. The style of your words—your syntax, your degree of formality, your grammar, and more—becomes a form of communication, and that style can make or break you in the working world.

Martin, for example, was not having trouble with words when he went to his boss to get the thumbs-up on whether he should buy that car he had his eye on. They were both speaking the same language—no gaps in dialect, no great divide between understanding that when Martin said he wanted to buy a car he was actually asking about his job security. Jack understood exactly what Martin was asking, but only Jack knows why he chose the indirect route to deal with Martin. As a result, while Martin and Jack both spoke the same language (English with a Texas twang), they used two distinct styles of communication.

Martin was really asking the question, "Look, man, I haven't been at this job long, and I'm uncertain about how you feel about me. If you think I'm good at what I do, let me know. If you're having problems with my work, shoot me a hint or, better yet, tell me straight I'm not cutting it." It was irrelevant that Martin was asking about buying a car. He could have mentioned buying a house, buying a puppy, or proposing to his girlfriend. The point was that by tying his new purchase to concerns about his job, Martin was asking his boss to give him feedback before he sank money he couldn't afford into a new ride.

Because Martin was a friend of mine, over the course of his employment he had confided in me his sense that his boss wasn't impressed with his work or work ethic. Therefore, it wasn't like he didn't have a clue that his job could have been on the line. I know that Jack's lack of directness was not entirely his fault. Martin was not good at reading his environment. While whites in general may not be as direct as blacks, if you pay attention, you can read loud and clear when someone is being indirect.

Jack had repeatedly made passing snide comments about Martin's failure to get to work on time. Jack had also commented a few times on problems he had with Martin's work. Martin may have thought he was being direct when he asked Jack about his performance, using the car-purchase issue as a way to soften the question, but that's not effective. Martin should have known that was not effective when Jack's response addressed the car-purchase issue and did *not* address the performance issue. At that point, Martin should have more directly asked about his work performance, or he should have just held off on buying the car until he got his official evaluation. In Martin's case, the 15 percent difference regarding that particular conversation might not have prevented him from losing his job in the first place, but it might have saved him acquiring a new car note until he got his next job.

A study done on *intercultural sensitivity* (how different ethnic groups understand each other and get along) by Milton Bennett shows that there are six stages of development. Although the model is based on the premise that whites are the ones who need to learn intercultural sensitivity, the model actually applies to a person of color trying to make his or her way in a workplace filled primarily with those from another culture.

The first stage is *denial*, where people do not recognize cultural differences. The second stage is *defense*, where people recognize some differences but see them as negative. The third stage is *minimization*, where people are unaware of their projection of their own cultural values onto others and see their own values as superior. Stage four is *acceptance*, where people shift their perspectives to understand that what they consider ordinary behavior can have different meanings in different cultures.

Adaptation, which is stage five, involves evaluating the behavior of people in a different cultural group from their frame of reference and adapting your behavior to fit what is normal in this different culture. The last stage of Bennett's theory is called *integration*, where people can shift their frames of reference and become comfortable with evaluating situations from multiple frames. Bennett's theory is instructive, because it points to the fact that when you enter a situation where the people are different from you, at some point you've got to adapt to the environment. While the environment may alter slightly because of the element that is different from the rest, it will basically remain the same.

Almost every black person has experienced a white person telling a story about some situation in which the white person was in the minority—visiting a black neighborhood or a black church or a meeting where most of the people attending were black. It's always amusing to hear the awe in white people's voices when they talk about their walk on the other side. It's usually very amusing to hear their pride in stating how they adapted to a "foreign" environment that, at best, they stayed in for an hour or two, max. We as blacks hearing those stories get either mad at or amused by the fact that whites don't make the connection that our adaptation happens every day we go to work.

Denial Ain't Just a River in Africa

Denial isn't a problem blacks generally have when we enter the workforce. Our parents probably expend far more effort and time emphasizing how different white folks are from us than white folks do with their own kids about blacks. In both cases, the differences emphasized are usually negative and not necessarily based on fact. In a nutshell, you can't teach what you don't know, so sometimes what gets passed down from one generation to the next are just untested stereotypes. Teaching blind negativity does not result in helpful tools.

Blacks who are survivors, depending on why they are emphasizing survival, usually focus on how whites are similar. Whites who work with black survivors usually knock themselves out encouraging them to downplay their differences, allowing those blacks to emphasize similarities so that they don't have to step out of their comfort zones.

Strivers, like survivors, recognize the areas of similarity, but they emphasize select areas for strategic purposes. Although some may be clumsy at it while others are skilled, black strivers usually know full well what they're doing when they emphasize the right things in communication. For example, a striver, hearing that his boss likes tennis, might make a point of interjecting tennis news or information into their casual interactions to signal, "I should get points, because we like the same thing." This differs from a survivor in that the striver is consciously trying to better her position with that particular boss by emphasizing similarities rather than simply trying to blend in as much as possible, which is more of the survivor's motivation.

Thrivers normally don't think about the impact their communication has on whites, because they don't care. A thriver, however, would be better served by paying more attention to the results of his communication to see if that attitude really serves him or where and when it doesn't. For example, if he finds his style of communication with his supervisor always leaves the supervisor acting defensive toward him, maybe that thriver needs to soften the way he communicates. In doing so, maybe he will increase his chances of getting more of what he wants and needs at work, from more money to better assignments to a more peaceful environment.

Blacks who are successful in the workplace know that communication and language are the key issues that are most likely to make that 15 percent difference rear its head. One of the ways a black person can minimize any difficulties in that respect is to do more listening than assuming.

One of the things I was infamous for at work was getting witnesses to talk to me and tell me things no one else could get out of them. Young, old, black, white, accused, accusers—I just have this knack for getting people to feel comfortable with me and tell me more than they plan to. From watching other people, particularly my white coworkers, conduct interviews, I think that what I do differently from most others that makes people more open with me is to not let my preconceived assumptions guide what I'm hearing. That allows me to hear what the person is saying, which leads to a better next question. For example, while I was interviewing a female employee who was accusing a male coworker of sexually harassing her, she mentioned in passing her friendship with another male coworker. Some instinct told me to probe her on the nature of this seemingly irrelevent friendship. She stumbled around with the answer, but the bottom line was she had a sexual relationship with him, and he was a good buddy of the accused. While technically that didn't absolve the accused of liability, it put her accusations in a different light, which later resulted in the complaint being dropped.

My point is that most people would have been so focused on eliciting information regarding the person she was actually making the complaint against that they wouldn't have bothered to ask about something seemingly irrelevant. I guess even as an attorney, the newspaper reporter in me is always pushed to ask the next nosy-ass question. Most people are so drenched in assumptions that they don't really hear other people. They hear the words but not the point. They hear the emotion, but they don't get the underlying concern. We all have a tendency to be more poised for rebuttal than we are open to hearing someone else's viewpoint.

In the workplace, you have to listen to people and observe them without judgment from day one. Studies say that most communication is nonverbal, and I believe that is true. Therefore, listening and watching the environment you work in is a way to better figure out communication. In general, you do that by listening to what your coworkers talk about, reading your environment for the use of idiom and expression, and paying attention to the style in which people speak. For example, as an 85 percent issue, if you work in a place where people curse like sailors, a well-chosen expletive won't damn you (pardon the pun). But if you rarely hear cussing at work, you might want to put a lid on that potty mouth in the office if you're aiming to be a driver.

Just Bring Up Tiger

One of the things that you listen for in the workplace is what people talk about. The arrival of Tiger Woods probably did more to bridge any 15 percent differences in communication than any other sports figure. Suddenly, it became cool for a black person to come to work talking about golf without sounding like he was straining too hard to talk to whites. (Of course, after Thanksgiving weekend 2009, bringing up Tiger Woods in the workplace could trigger a whole mess of controversial conversations about his predilection for white women in addition to his white wife, but Tiger as merely a golfer has always provided a great conversational bridge between blacks and whites in the workplace.)

Thrivers without a doubt will be the black employees who make the least allowance for different modes of communication by culture. A thriver will talk about the joys of the latest NBA draft picks while everyone else salutes Tiger Woods. A thriver will say "dis" and "dat" to the CEO with the same straightforwardness with which she talks to the clerk in the mailroom.

Under the paradigm stated by Bennett, the thrivers will never get to stage six—integration. Well, that's not true. Thrivers may have the ability to integrate—that is, they may recognize all the different ways to switch between cultures—but they just choose not to do so. Again, my classifications are about motivation, not ability. I know of one brother, a partner at a major, predominantly white law firm, who was educated at great schools but who deliberately turned up his black lingo around other white partners to force them to loosen up. He was instinctively a thriver; however, his success as a driver came from (1) being stellar in his area of practice, and (2) knowing when it was safer to trot out the black patois and when circumstances, such as meeting with a client or being in court, required him to flash the Ivy League smile and speak King's English.

Code Switching

Code switching—the term used to describe being bicultural (operating simultaneously in two different cultures)—is just something most blacks have to learn from the time we leave our parents' homes to go out into the world. Another term I've heard used to describe code switching is *functional multilingualism.* An example of that is saying "Excuse me" when you accidentally bump into a white coworker and reflexively saying "My bad" when you accidentally bump into a black coworker later that day. Granted, both of your coworkers might refer to you as a klutz, but that would just be an example of how most cultures intersect.

We all code switch to a certain degree. For example, in my home, I own a "refrigerator." When I go over to a friend's home, regardless of his or her race, I refer to the appliance in the kitchen as a "refrigerator." But when I walk into my grandmother's house and head for the kitchen, suddenly the only word I know for the electric contraption that keeps food cold is "icebox." That's what I grew up hearing, that's what Cliffie (my grandmother) still calls it, and that's the word I revert to when I visit her house. Code switching isn't just about race; it's about environment and reverting back to comfort and habit. That's why you'll be talking with a second generation coworker or friend who doesn't have a trace of an accent, and you'll see her get a call from a relative where she immediately falls into another language. Then she'll hang up and, without missing a beat, resume her conversation in English with you. I love that! Unfortunately, when blacks do that, it's called one of my least favorite words—*Ebonics*.

Language is such a rich, vivid part of who we are. Even the way different cultures use the same words can say so much about them. Cedric the Entertainer talks about how the difference between blacks and whites is the difference between wishing and hoping. Whites will run late for a concert saying, "I hope no one is sitting in our seats." Blacks will run late for a concert and say, "I wish someone would be sitting in our seats." Granted, on paper, it doesn't have the same tone, the same resonance, the same kick-ass attitude with which Cedric says it, but we all know what he means.

How We Say It Is How We Live It

The original title of my book was *Flavor in the Melting Pot: The Black Person's Guide to Employment in the White World*. The publishers changed it because they didn't think the title was descriptive enough for what the book was about. I agree; however, this expression is how I think of us—as the flavor that makes the melting pot stew richer, tastier.

There's a reason why black words and phrases make their way into everyday language. I think I fell off my couch the first time I heard a white television character say "It's all good" like he grew up with some colored people. That's our stuff. Our words. We know the phrases that unite us. Words like "If he had been black and done that" or "We can't keep nothing for ourselves." Black employees say those words whenever it applies or wherever they can say it without being overheard. Sometimes we don't have to say the words. We can just glance across a room during a meeting or across a piece of equipment at each other, and the words get said without speaking. We get tired of having to validate our experiences, and so we keep them to ourselves, which just increases the conversations and reactions we have behind the backs of whites. Understand that my point is not that these comments and conversations happen every day, but yep, they happen frequently and they happen regardless of class.

I think white coworkers, bosses, customers, and subordinates don't realize there are a whole host of words, phrases, and catchwords that form a universal sublanguage or shorthand. We all know what a "HNIC" (Head N**** in Charge) is, and we've all heard the adage about how we (meaning blacks) have to get up earlier in the morning to be able to go toe-to-toe with whites. And there is no question that we've heard about the "crabs in the barrel" syndrome in which one black contends with other blacks trying to bring him down from success.

We black people need to do the bilingual thing. To do that successfully we have to start really listening to how whites talk and communicate with each other. It also means that we have to pay attention to how whites don't communicate with each other.

If Martin were operating from survivor mode, his best bet would have been to just not ask his boss about his status and wait until he received his official evaluation. Survivors should assume that white managers will be as risk averse as they are toward direct confrontation, and for people who operate from a passive-aggressive posture, any conversation past "Hello, how are you doing today?" becomes a breeding ground for confrontation.

A striver probably would have asked in a less direct fashion. For example, a striver might have said, "Hey, Jack, I'm really interested in getting feedback on my job performance, and I'm interested in knowing what role you see me playing in the future with this organization. Can we sit down and talk about that?" A striver would be operating with a dual agenda—the agenda of figuring out where he really stood with his boss while also genuinely wanting to know if he had enough job security to acquire a new debt.

A thriver probably wouldn't have asked at all, because if he wanted a new car he would have bought one. He wouldn't have given the boss even the illusion he had any power over that decision.

Some things blacks just can't change overnight. Dialect is one of them. I sound like a black woman from the Midwest, educated in primarily white schools. Someone meeting me for the first time would guess that I'm educated, but they wouldn't mistake me either for a preppie or as coming directly from the 'hood. If I tried to sound like either extreme, I would just sound silly. Because I work in the Midwest, my dialect isn't an issue.

How your accent or dialect sounds in your workplace is something that you need to be conscious of if it is different from the rest. The bottom line is that as a black person, if you work in any kind of professional job, you have to get the basics of proper English down pat. Regardless of whether you are a survivor, a striver, or a thriver, you need to make sure your subjects and verbs agree in your sentences. If you're in the habit of dissing and datting too much (translation: mispronouncing "this" and "that"), you need to get it under control. You need to be bilingual enough to control it when you're at work at least.

Communication is also more than how you say things; it's also the subjects you choose to talk about. The following is my list of no-no topics at work, no matter what type of employee you are:

- Any white artist accused of stealing from black pop culture
- Affirmative action
- Politics (especially the role that race played in the election of President Obama and the role it plays in criticism of how he performs as president)
- Welfare
- Poverty
- Crime
- Living in the suburbs (unless you're a black who lives in the suburbs)
- Anything relating to sex
- The problem with racial profiling

I could list about ten other off-limits topics, but everyone has to use his own judgment based on his particular job. You may be wondering what you can talk about. Until you know your environment and the boundaries you have with individual coworkers, safe, non-work-related topics include sports, pop culture events, nonpolitical news events, general family topics, and the weather. The weather is always a safe topic.

Regardless of whether you are a survivor, striver, or thriver, here are some principles that can help you to succeed with workplace communication and keep any 15 percent difference issues to a minimum.

First of all, while there are some jobs that don't involve any writing at all (such as manual labor jobs), being particularly conscious of writing well is a necessity. When you write e-mails, memorandums, anything, you have to demonstrate your grasp of English. It may be an unfair standard, but we can't afford to appear any more uneducated than some stereotypes indicate we are, particularly if we are strivers or work in any kind of job where a degree is required. If you think you have problems with basic writing, you should hunt out a friend you trust and who you think is a good writer and ask for help. If you're uncomfortable with that approach, buy a book on good writing or take a class at the community college. The important issue is not whether white folks think you're a good writer but whether you have the confidence to know that you are communicating at your best at all times.

Most word processing programs allow you to check the spelling and grammar on documents. Do it. Do it before you send an e-mail so that even if you don't sound overly educated, you at least come off as careful—an extremely important attribute to be known for, no matter what your job is. In addition to using spell check, keeping a dictionary or a thesaurus handy is also a good idea.

Another tip is to observe how the people around you communicate, especially the people who have the greatest impact on your job. Listen to how people talk to others, and then compare that to what they say when those people aren't around. Observe whom your bosses go out of their way to talk to when it is not directly job related, and objectively pay attention to why they do so. Don't just get caught up in the knee-jerk reaction of "My white boss only talks to white people," because usually it isn't that simple. I once made that assumption about a boss. He was a white male in his fifties, and at social events I noticed that he appeared to go out of his way to talk only to the other white men. It used to really piss me off, but when I stepped back and thought about it, I noticed that it wasn't all the white males that he talked to. So I started paying greater attention to his conversations with the white males he did talk to. What I noticed was that his main topic of conversation with them was sports and that the white males he didn't talk to were not big sports fans. Bingo! Well, after I started throwing the occasional sports metaphor into my conversation and striking up chats about certain sporting events, he began loosening up around me. We started having a better, more open working relationship in general. Now granted, my initial instinct was right—he gravitated more toward white men because his unstated bias was that those guys would have more in common with him. But my objective was to have a better working relationship with him, not to undo fifty years of bias that existed before he met me.

After you've observed your environment, act accordingly. If you are a big user of slang and you see that others you work with aren't, keep it to a minimum, except for conversations with coworkers you're very tight and personal with. It's also important to moderate your pitch and tone. If you work in a dry, low-key environment, then don't be the loudest person in the room. (I've always had trouble with that one too, but life is easier when I pay attention and attempt to bring it down a notch in those environments.) Trust me, if you're black and you're loud when everyone else is a soft talker, somehow that will bite you in the butt.

You also need to know what *not* to communicate. Unless you work in an environment where the nature of the job involves openly talking about racial issues, as a black person it's just best to stay away from such *scary* conversations at work. (My definition of *scary* is any topic that draws attention to the fact that you're black and other people in the room aren't.) It's a no-win situation. Now granted, if you're a thriver, accustomed to doing things your way without regard to perception, then it doesn't matter. If the water cooler discussion turns to how *Seinfeld* was one of the greatest television shows ever made and you want to point out that you don't understand how a show demonstrating life in New York City didn't have any black folks in it, bring it on—but when the comfort level suddenly turns icy, know that's the chance you take.

Communication is one of the most important ways you need to attend to your 15 percent issues if you want to successfully get yours and get ahead at work. If you train yourself to read your environment automatically, however, it's easier than you think.

5

HAIR, FLAIR, AND WHAT YOU WEAR

■

Mark pledged Omega Psi Pi fraternity when he was an undergrad at the University of Everybody's Business. Just about every black college student knows that part of pledging Omega Psi Pi, also known as the Qs, may mean more than handing over your money and wearing purple and gold. As part of his "going over" (as pledging is called), Mark got the infamous *Q* branded on his arm. Branded. Hot iron. Imprinted, bold and huge, on the bicep of his right arm. The brand may not take up much space, but there's no avoiding it once you see his bare arm.

Fast forward a few years later to when this young, upstanding brother was a second-year law student with a summer clerkship at a conservative, all-white law firm. Mark found himself invited to several swimming pool party events—the kind of socializing that is particularly important for black folks so that the people who are hiring can figure out if you know how to use the right fork in front of clients or make appropriate small talk without embarrassing yourself or the firm.

Needless to say, Mark didn't get in the pool that summer. He made sure his T-shirts carefully covered his beloved brand. Covering it up was physically not that hard to do; the average sleeve on a T-shirt would do. Unfortunately, his nervousness while trying to make sure no one saw the brand at all those "casual" outdoor firm events made Mark seem standoffish and socially inept.

Mark did a good job that summer; however, he wasn't offered a full-time position when the summer was over.

Moral of the story? Don't try to get a job at an all-white law firm if you're not white? No. Don't join fraternities or sororities that require body parts to be altered or permanently imprinted? Well, that would get into my personal opinion. The true moral of the story is that, like communication, physical appearance is something all workers need to be concerned with. It can also be one of the first areas to see the 15 percent factor creep in.

Part of being black in the white workplace involves understanding that you may be the first and only black that your coworkers, bosses, and subordinates deal with on a daily basis. From the day you start, it doesn't take a psychic to read which of your white workmates deal with blacks up close and personal only when they are at work. That's why appearance can be a form of communication. We judge other people, whether fairly or not, by how they carry themselves. For example, we draw different conclusions about a woman who has six pairs of holes in her ears versus a woman who only wears clip-on pearl earrings. Even a person who has no idea who Lil' Kim is will not look at a picture of her and assume she's a schoolteacher. More likely, a person seeing a picture of Lil' Kim wearing a tight, bright, and see-through outfit would appropriately guess that she was an entertainer.

Appearance can be our calling card. Never is that more important than when interviewing for a job. While being yourself is important, presenting that self in the best light should be your number-one priority.

The basics always apply:

- Make sure you look clean and neat.
- Don't wear an outfit to an interview that you would wear to a nightclub.
- Gum in any flavor or mode of chewing is out.
- Ball caps or tennis shoes aren't for the office.
- Try to limit your aroma to soap, because you never know when your interviewer has a perfume or cologne allergy.
- There is no such thing as "off the record" when it comes to job hunting. Even if you're just going to pick up an application or drop off a letter of reference, make sure your appearance reflects your serious interest in the job.

Once when I was in the office of a human resources manager during the investigation of a case I worked on, a brother came in off the street to ask for a job application. I couldn't see the man from where I was sitting, but I could hear the disdain in the manager's voice as she asked him questions and gave him an application. The manager, a young black woman, told me that it annoyed her when black people came in for an application looking "any ol' way." Apparently the young man must have worked at a job that involved plenty of dark, oily grease, because his body and clothes were smudged all over with it.

While that young man may have stopped for an application during the only time he could—on his way home from the job he already had—his appearance worked against him. You don't have to dress up as if you are meeting the CEO on every encounter, but until you have the starting date of a new job, assume that every appearance you make counts. (And don't ever discount the people who work in human resources, because what they lack in power, they usually make up for in influence and access when you're trying to get the job in the first place.)

Like any other group, we take for granted that our style of doing things is something that everyone knows about. For example, we assume that everyone knows that we don't have to wash our hair every day. We assume that when we say we're going to get a permanent, that means our hair comes back straighter, not curlier as it does for whites. We take for granted that when we're invited to a party and told that the dress is casual, that means we go a little tighter, a little brighter, and definitely a little bolder.

Never underestimate how the language of dress screams. If you wear orange every day in a sea of blue suits, you signal more than that you like the color orange. You show your employers that you are bold, original, and unconventional. Look at the cues around you, however. If no one else is being bold, you might stand out as eccentric. At the very least, if you're going to wear the orange every day over your black skin, you better excel beyond the best of the blue suits at what you do. That's where researching your environment before you get the job becomes especially necessary.

Once you get an interview, use that as your opportunity to pay careful attention to the appearance of the people at the company. Note if hairdos are conservative or funky. Observe if clothes are sedate or stand out. Watch to see if people wear offbeat jewelry or strictly stick to Timex and gold studs. Being aware of these things when you interview will show you if more than just your wardrobe clashes with your work environment.

Let's get back to Mark for a minute. First of all, let's ask, was he trying to survive, strive, or thrive? Assume that Mark was trying to survive. When you're clerking for the purpose of getting a job, your only real goal is getting the job offer at the end of the proverbial rainbow. You can pretend in your mind that if you get the job you will start on your first day of work wearing a five-foot-high Afro and a "No Justice, No Peace" T-shirt and greeting all your coworkers with an appropriate Muslim greeting. (You know you're not going to do that, but little mental daydreams like that may be what get you through the rough spots.) As someone aiming to survive, Mark would be smart to wear a T-shirt over his brand, keep a low profile, and take his chances. There was no way, when he was spending the summer trying to get a job, that he needed to have conversations with white folks on why a black man would willingly get himself branded. Any conversation a black person gets himself into at work that even remotely touches on slavery (as branding would) is a no-win situation.

Now, say Mark was trying to strive—get the job offer but not feel like he had to hide in the shadows to do so. If that were the case, then Mark's approach would be a little different. One, he probably would still just keep the T-shirt on for all outdoor events. But as someone striving, he would probably have a personality that allowed him to court the white folks a little bit more. In other words, he would reach out more to get to know folks individually and take the extra time to strike up conversations on things he had in common with others so that people paid less attention to the fact that he was not jumping his seminaked butt in the pool.

On the other hand, if Mark were trying to thrive, well, then he probably wouldn't have to boost his T-shirt collection before his clerkship started. He probably would not care what the white folks thought, because his loyalty to his fraternity or just his own sense of integrity about not hiding anything about himself would rule. It would still be wise for Mark, Q brand and all, to extend himself and explain his fraternity's philosophy about the branding and why members willingly subject themselves to a hot iron. There will be that slice of white folks who will find it fascinating and educational, and they might even bond with Mark as they bring up their own crazy college antics. Then there will be that group of white folks who won't have the guts to get into an actual discussion with Mark about it. They will write him off as a radical Negro or ex–gang member, and they'll either keep him from getting the job or be a problem once he gets it anyway.

One thing is for sure. Whether Mark aimed to survive, strive, or thrive, lying is never an option in the workplace, especially for blacks. In a nutshell, Mark's options were to cover up his brand, reframe how the brand came about, or just refuse to talk about it and hope for the best.

There are two reasons why I don't suggest lying, even about something as seemingly minor as a fraternity symbol. I'm a believer in operating with integrity at all times. If you wanted to be a Q dog more than you wanted air to breathe when you were in college, then you shouldn't be ashamed of the fact that you were willing to get a brand. Discreetly hiding it from your employers is not the same as hiding it from yourself, which is what you do when you lie about it. We've all got things from our past that we are either ashamed of or, at the very least, not proud of, but lying about an aspect of your past is just too high a price to pay for getting any job. When you get your dream job, as a black person, you don't want any skeletons jumping out of your closets, even little bitty skeletons. This same analysis applies whether we're talking about a brand, tattoo, piercing, or hairstyle—anything you don't want to or can't hide for personal reasons.

As a former employment attorney I can advise you not to lie, because lies almost always come to light. Stick to the high road; then if you ever have to pursue any action against your boss, you have truth on your side and don't have to worry about your credibility flushing your case down the toilet. Bottom line is, blacks just don't have the option to have credibility issues in the workplace. Even an empty lie, such as saying that your fraternity brothers wrestled you to the ground and gave you the brand, has a way of catching up with you. When I worked as a newspaper reporter I learned that there is always someone who knows the truth to any lie you tell. And as a lawyer who has investigated discrimination lawsuits, I've learned that there is always someone willing to tell that truth under oath in a deposition.

One aspect about dress that many people, blacks in particular, don't think about is that while how you carry yourself communicates who you are and what you want, the way employees dress and conduct their grooming to a certain extent communicates the objective of the employer.

Take McDonald's, for example. We do more than recognize those golden arches. No one would deny McDonald's has the right to require employees to wear uniforms to work with no significant deviations. We would all probably agree that the company has the right to convey a unified corporate image so that people get the same comfort level whether they're at a Mickey D's in Rochester, New York, or Rolla, Missouri, or Riverside, California.

Even in an environment where uniforms are not required, companies have the right to set a standard and tone that convey a certain type of professionalism. While blacks have brought lawsuits against their employers for grooming policies that they felt were discriminatory, such as prohibiting black men from wearing beards to cover up keloid scars or black women from wearing braids (other than when Bo Derek made them fashionable, that is), that's a hard road to go down if your bottom line is to keep your job. Besides, it's easier to complain about a policy prohibiting bushy Afros than a policy that prohibits you from wearing your Bootsy Collins and P-Funk concert T-shirt to work as an accountant.

If you want to be a driver, you need to make grooming choices that are not just about your personal taste but about maximizing the image you present to anyone you meet as an employee—whether customer, client, vendor, stockholder, or member of the public. Even when you don't have hard-and-fast rules to follow, make the choices that not only make you look good but make you look good in the way it really counts.

Fred is a brother who has been a newspaper reporter for almost fifteen years. On any given day Fred could be called to any assignment at any time in any part of the city. When it came to how he presented himself physically, Fred was a driver right down to his polished shoes. He knew that to convince anyone to talk to an unknown black man, he needed to wear clothes that put people at ease. Fred found that a tie, pressed shirt, and khakis or suitable dress pants (plus a reporter's notebook) usually eased his way through any threshold.

Sure, there were times when Fred wanted to skip the tie or not pull out the iron. There were times when Fred wanted to wear a T-shirt to beat the heat or a sweatshirt that was comfy when it was too damn cold. There were days when he just plain didn't feel like pulling out razor. But he knew those weren't options. He put himself in charge of driving his career forward, and he knew that the first time a source or witness refused to be interviewed by him because she was wary of his appearance, the burden would be on him to explain to his bosses why he didn't get the story.

Of course, there were times when people didn't speak to Fred anyway—that's a professional hazard for any journalist—but

Fred knew that his appearance was his first calling card, even before he identified himself. He couldn't afford ever to forget that if he wanted front-page news stories, he needed always to look the part.

Sometimes though, the 15 percent issue becomes the 100 percent issue.

Julia was an administrative assistant in a small company where she was the only black. She had always done a great job— her boss raved about her work publicly and in her reviews, which always led to hefty raises. Julia decided, as many millions of black women have, that the chemical relaxer in her hair was just too much for her—too much money, too much effort, too much chemical slapped on her scalp. When she got all the new growth cut out of her hair, leaving enough natural hair to make stylish twists, she was stunned to come to work and have her boss bluntly tell her that he found her new hairstyle "scary." Sometimes, in some places, a black person will meet with the inconvenience of someone else's stereotype no matter how hard she works.

The key issue is awareness. You have to be aware that apparent differences merit discussion, conversation, and spotlights. Sometimes you feel like being an educator, sometimes you don't. One of the realities is that our uniqueness in being black and our desire to be unique among our brothers and sisters sometimes makes our grooming a topic of conversation.

Mary the JD, my friend at work, made some changes over a six-month period of time: she went from having her hair as short as Halle Berry to having shoulder-length braids à la Brandy to hair that was Toni Braxton straight when Toni was in her long-mane phase. Did girlfriend care what the white folks thought about the fact that she went through almost as many looks as

Mary J. Blige does between the Grammys and the Soul Train Awards? Nope. But the important thing my friend was aware of before she did it is that the one thing that merits more attention than difference is change. Therefore, Mary the JD was prepared for the attention, and she knew that her work environment was relaxed enough to accept personal expression. She knew all of this *before* she made the changes so that she could smoothly and appropriately handle any hair-focused discussions.

Mary also kept the topic of her hair care off the debating team schedule in the first place. I've seen my African American sisters launch loud campaigns about their color, cut, or addition to their hair while at work. Unfortunately, some of us give the appearance of putting more thought into our hair and clothes than we do into our jobs or our careers. An overstatement? Look at the facts. African Americans spend three times as much on cosmetics as the rest of America. Yep. We spend money on looking good, and as part of looking good, we draw attention to ourselves. That's great, because a sister doesn't put on a hot new lip color to not look good. A brother does not have his barber shave him just right to not look tight.

White people like to look good, too. I know of one white coworker who is legendary for going to the barber to get his hair trimmed more often than most of us floss our teeth. That's not the point. The point is that success in the workplace requires that more attention be paid to how well you do your job than to how fashionable you look doing it. We, by the very nature of being black in the workplace, generate more attention, and one thing we all know is that, for some reason, what we do gets blown up to the size of a big-screen television when we do it.

Anna has a small tattoo on the inside of one of her wrists. She had a great interview with her employer, but for reasons unknown to Anna, the employer required a background check based on her concern that the tattoo might represent a wild past that could have negative implications if Anna got the job. But she didn't have a wild past. She just had a tattoo—not the most strategically placed tattoo for someone climbing the corporate ladder, but, hey, for that particular job, it caused no more than a short delay and a questionable invasion of her privacy that she never found out about.

So what's the answer? You've got to wear clothes to work. Your hair has to look some way. Tattoos or fraternity brands may already be part of your personal mix.

If you're a survivor, the answer is to keep it simple and keep it silent. This means that you keep your experimental hairdos and attention-grabbing styles for the weekend or vacation or until you reach the point in your career where you really don't care. Regardless of what you do, you observe what the corporate culture looks like and follow it as closely as your sun-kissed skin can comfortably get away with. Keep your grooming tips out of the workplace. If you work in a khaki-wearing, blue-shirt-sporting fashion palace, you break out the Dockers and act happy about it.

If you're a striver and you want to make your professional mark on the workplace while imbuing it with your own personal style, I still say keep it silent. Be fashionably elegant or breakout beautiful, but always keep the focus on how well you do your job and how good your work results are. Let your personal style just be one of those things that people notice but that doesn't attract undue attention.

The question for those who don't want to compromise nor be slaves to corporate culture is to just be aware of the consequences. For example, since the year 2000 I have had dreadlocks.

Back when I practiced law, many a jaw dropped when the attorney with dreadlocks who came in wasn't representing the person suing but representing the company being sued. I took the chance every day that some judge, some client, some witness, some person I worked with would jump to some sort of judgment about me based on my "radical" hairstyle. For me it was worth it because I really like my hair. Now, when I worked at the second-biggest law firm in the same city, my hair was permed and straight as a bone. There was no way my behind would even have gotten the job with any hairstyle that screamed ethnic. Would they have told me that's why I didn't get the job? Hell, no. I did work for lawyers. Would they have intentionally discriminated against me if I had started growing the locs while I was there? As a corporation, no. But there would have been some individual I worked for whose perception of me would have changed, and while the law does prohibit discrimination, it doesn't prohibit negative perceptions. That may be a fuzzy line, but it's the fuzzy line we live with. (See chapter 10 for more on this topic.)

The point of this chapter isn't really about fraternity brands or hairstyles. It's about how we wear our selves—our true selves—and how that plays in the workplace. A client I worked for, an employer of a large entry-level workforce, some time ago took a survey of its employees to design a fair dress-code policy so that the company didn't inadvertently fail to take into account some issue. What the survey revealed is that the young black female employees had much different standards of what was appropriate to wear to work than the white female employees did. The black women didn't have as much problem with lower necklines and higher hemlines. At least at this workplace, with those particular employees, flashing a little T and A wasn't such a bad thing. That particular employer cared enough about fairness to adjust its policies to take into account cultural and generational differences. Most employers don't. They have rules and standards that they expect employees to follow and bosses that aren't too skilled at custom-fitting the standard.

The main issue for us is awareness. The second issue is choice. The order of those two things is important. My mother is a high school graduate who has worked for the federal government for more than thirty years and has been promoted about a jillion times, gaining more supervisory duties and responsibility with every move. My mom is way ahead of me—starting with less and doing a heck of a lot more. One of her favorite responses when I tell her that this person did this or that person did that is just to say, "Choices. Everybody has them."

Awareness and choice go hand in hand in the workplace. Be aware of the possible outcomes or perceptions that could result from the choices you make. Being aware will help you evaluate your choices ahead of time so that you don't react to a given situation without forethought.

Lenny, an attorney, told me he would love to loc his hair, but he wouldn't because of the impact he feared this particular hair choice would have on his clients. Lenny's rationale was that while people may accept locs from a black female trial attorney as nothing more than a hairstyle choice, with a black man it would come across as some sort of social statement. Lenny demonstrated the power of how awareness must come before choice. In his case, he knew that he was not going to take a chance on something that would hurt not only him but also his clients. As a trial attorney in a fairly conservative and racially divided city, Lenny was aware that, while he had the choice to wear his hair any way he wanted, he had to read his environment well enough to decide how much he was and wasn't willing to risk with his personal choice.

Lenny wasn't an employee, since he had his own law firm, but even he knew that he had to play to his audience if he wanted success. Playing to his audience meant being aware of what would be acceptable, then making a choice based on that. At work, your audience is your boss, your coworkers, and your customers or clients.

A young black woman, Gina, called a colleague of mine— also a black employment lawyer—a few years ago to ask her if it was illegal for Gina's boss to tell her that the skirts she wore to work were too short. Gina just knew my friend was going to tell her, "Hell no, he can't do that! This is America, damn it, and he has no right to tell you what you can and can't wear. He's violating your civil rights. Let's sue the bastard!" Instead, what Gina got was my colleague telling her that since she was an at-will employee, her boss had the right to enforce an across-the-board, nondiscriminatory dress code that prevented employees from wearing clothes that were unduly distracting and thus inappropriate for the workplace.

Now my personal style, as opposed to that of my fellow sister litigator, would have been to tell Gina something along the lines of, if you show up at a conservative insurance company every day showing more leg than a Popeye's Chicken Snack Pack, then maybe you shouldn't be surprised when your boss says something to you about putting more clothes on. But that's my style.

Anyway you slice it, if Gina was more aware that her hemline was quite a bit shorter than every other woman's at work, then maybe she would have made a better choice, rather than having her boss call her out about something that could have been avoided. Now you may say at this point, maybe Gina wasn't trying to survive or even strive. Maybe Gina was trying to thrive. That's a good point, but that's why reading your environment is the key to success in your workplace. In Gina's environment, wearing butt-crack-high skirts may have been the breaking point where her individualism came head-to-head with the boss's ideal of workplace attire. Bottom line was, Gina was not the boss. She could crow all she wanted to about how it wasn't fair, but in the end it wasn't her call to make. Her choices were to get another job, break her own fashion rules and wear longer skirts, or take it to a higher authority at work and let that person or department decide. Calling an attorney was her way of figuring out what her options were. Gina was counseled that if she chose to go over her supervisor's head, that path is going to put the spotlight not just on her hemline but on her entire performance.

One thing you should look at when you accept a new job is if there is a dress code outlined in the company handbook. A company is not legally required to have a dress-code policy (actually a company doesn't even have to have a company handbook, but most do), but if they do, then you aren't going to have much room for deviation.

Everyone is going to have a hairstyle—even if the style is bald. And unless you work at a nudist colony, everyone has to figure out what to wear to work every day. But the growing trend of young people having more visible tattoos and piercings addresses two fashion statements that are a choice every time.

Tattoos have become more accepted today. People are used to more people having them and having them in more visible places. However, there is limit to how much an employer is willing to view tattoos in a positive, or at least neutral, light.

In 2007, Vault.com, a publisher of career matters, took a survey in which 85 percent of the respondents said they believe that tattoos and body piercings impede a person's chance of finding a job. One person wrote, "Regardless of who the real person may be, stereotypes associated with piercings and tattoos can and do affect others. In general, individuals with tattoos and body piercings are often viewed as 'rougher' or 'less educated.'"

In 2005, the Employment Law Alliance polled one thousand Americans, and 39 percent said that employers should have the right to deny employment to someone based on appearance, including weight, clothing, piercings, tattoos, and hairstyle. Even more significant, of that 39 percent who believe that appearance should be regulated by an employer, based on how the respondents identified themselves, whites outnumbered nonwhites 41 to 24 percent.

While a low number of employers have actual policies prohibiting visible tattoos and excessive piercings, I believe that number will grow as more people get offensive and inappropriate body art on visible parts of their bodies. At a recent Jamie Foxx concert, where I saw a large number of black men and women displaying tattoos that featured penises, curse words, and other "charming" representations, I seriously wondered where some of these folks worked, because many of the tattoos were in places that couldn't easily be covered up unless you wore a turtleneck sweater to work every day.

The issue, as it should be, is one of judgment. For example, a butterfly on an ankle of a woman applying to be an administrative assistant won't be a deal breaker at most places (although to be on the safe side, she should wear stockings to decrease attention to it if applying at a conservative company). However, an "R.I.P. Pookie" tattooed across the front of the neck probably will be something that will make the average hiring person pause. Therefore, while tattoos may be more accepted by society, employers still seek people who show good judgment. Whether folks like it or not, excessive, graphic tattoos on anyone besides an NBA star, a hip-hop artist, or the owner of a tattoo parlor will probably not put you on top of the "to be hired" list.

Now piercings are a different story. I had a contract to be the human resources consultant for a small nursing home facility a few years ago, where I was involved in the hiring and training of new employees. This nursing home was in a black neighborhood where most of the residents were black; thus most of the employees and job applicants were also black. I was amazed at the large number of young women—I'm not talking one or two here—applying for nursing assistant jobs who had tongue piercings. These were young women who often had the training or the experience to do difficult, admirable work with the elderly and infirm but who didn't have the judgment to realize how a piercing was not only distracting to look at but also affected their ability to speak, which are two things you do not want to unnecessarily have happen in the work environment.

A tattoo, depending on where it is placed, may be something that you have to live with. But before you get a job investigate whether your piercings are personal statements that you should choose to take out if in visible places not including your ears.

Whether whites want to admit it or not, when blacks show up in the workplace what we do, say, or wear takes on big-screen, Technicolor drama, while what every other employee does, says, or wears gets displayed on the thirteen-inch screen. If you're aware, then you pay attention to your environment and make choices about where you as a black person fit in and what you accomplish in that environment. Whether your goal is to survive, strive, or thrive, isn't that what it's all about—doing well and living well while you're doing it?

In a nutshell, blacks do our "stuff" differently. We bring not just race but color to the workplace—different hair colors, bright colors, sharp colors, the colors of the rainbow, and the vivid colors of our minds. Awareness of how we look doing it is just another layer we constantly need to evaluate in our pursuit of cash and career.

6

WHAT THE $%^& ARE
YOU TWEETING?

■

Dwight had two college degrees in a field where jobs were plentiful, even in a down economy. For some reason, however, Dwight couldn't close the deal on a job, even though he considered himself a personable guy with a good resume. When he asked my opinion on what the problem was, I suggested that he take a good look at his public MySpace page and that he look at it through the eyes of a prospective employer.

Dwight was skeptical that this could be the problem, reasoning that even if employers looked, it was his personal business. I pointed out that Dwight was looking to get in a field involving public money and social welfare, yet his MySpace page detailed (and I mean *detailed*) heavy social drinking, graphic escapades with women, extensive party-

ing, and belligerent political commentary about Republicans
when we were still working with a Republican presidency.
Dwight switched his setting to private. Shortly afterward,
he found a job in his field. Coincidence? Maybe. But maybe
his making it a little more difficult to find out just how much
he partied like a rock star was the smartest advice he ever
took.

Even more than having a black president or a deep recession,
one of the biggest social revolutions of the past few years has
been the evolution of social networking—Facebook, Twitter,
BlackPlanet, MySpace, YouTube, Tagged, podcasts, Web sites I
haven't even heard of yet, Web sites that are constantly being
invented. Nielsen Online found that the number of minutes
Americans spent on social networks grew 83 percent from April
2008 to April 2009, with the total number of minutes spent on
Facebook increasing 700 percent in that same time period.

The issues that the rise of these popular sites have created for
employers—and thus black employees—are growing with each
new site created and as the existing sites increase in popularity.
The biggest issue is that of privacy and what prospective and current employers can discover about you. Finland bans employers
from Googling prospective employees before hiring them. Lucky
Finns. Here in America there is no such ban, and our cultural
mores make that kind of move highly unlikely any time soon.

One of the key things to remember for anyone "working
while black" is that what separates our experience from those of
our white and other nonblack counterparts isn't that anything

between us is factually different but that many times it is experienced differently. The use of social networking is a key example: the issue isn't that there are certain sites directed just at blacks versus sites that target the majority culture. Yes, there are Web sites called BlackPlanet and AOL Black Voices that cater to black Internet users. But blacks have to have profile names, passwords, and answers to secret questions in case the login information is forgotten, just like they do at any Web site primarily haunted by white people.

Social networking, for blacks, is just a sophisticated version of coffeepot chatter at work and full-scale networking at conferences, conventions, and workshops that blacks have to pack a briefcase or suitcase to attend. The point is that social networking has the blessing of providing ways for blacks to communicate, vent, and inquire in greater numbers and greater speed—but with more danger that those who are not in the proverbial conversation might "overhear" what we have to say.

In black communication and oral tradition, there's a term called "call-and-response"—it is a back-and-forth in blacks' communication style that is more fluid, interactive, and vocal. In many ways, that is how social networking differs for black Americans. While whites and others use the same devices and Web sites to comment, many blacks use social networking as a modern day call-and-response—a comment posted about a racist incident or a public figure or an issue particularly close to the heart of blacks might elicit several comments saying nothing more than some version of, "Tell it!" "Preach!" or "I know that's right."

Again, the difference for blacks in addressing the issue of social networking isn't about the medium itself being different, it's about how the issues that arise from using it affect blacks differently. Just like three blacks standing at a watercooler can draw extra attention in certain predominantly white workplaces, so can having the same conversation via public Facebook postings or message-board postings that can be traced to your work account. But it can have potentially greater consequences because you let your guard down, thinking that what you are saying and how you are saying it is personal.

Here are a few examples of some of the consequences in the workplace involving social networking sites:

- Florida, Colorado, Tennessee, and Massachusetts have released or suspended teachers over the content of their MySpace pages.

- In 2009 two New Jersey employees sued their former employer after they were fired for their MySpace activities in which they made fun of their supervisors and coworkers.

- A recent survey found that 17 percent of large employers have disciplined employees for social networking activities and 8 percent of large employers have terminated employees for social networking activities.

- A woman was fired for leaving work after saying that she had a migraine and couldn't use her computer but was then caught posting on her Facebook page later that day.

Even though this is the country that likes to trumpet free speech, it's beyond naive to think that prospective employers are not going to use the easiest, most accessible free tool for checking on a prospective employee to see just how freely they speak and how they might represent the company. It's also naive to think that employers or individual managers won't use the Internet to check on current employees.

It's particularly naive to think that employers won't take advantage of something that's free and readily accessible on the very desks they sit at every day. Remember *WWW* stands for *World Wide Web*. And if you are a black candidate applying for a job with someone who may have a problem hiring blacks, or if you give off a vibe that person doesn't like, then for sure the employer will Google you faster than you can pose and have your friend tell you "Say cheese."

Like Dwight, you can fool yourself that your personal business is just that, but your judgment, or lack thereof, will be grounds for not hiring you. And if what you post is salacious enough, it won't trip any discrimination wires.

If you read the news, you will occasionally hear of teachers or folks working in sensitive fields getting fired for having naughty pictures on their Facebook pages or the pages of some other social networking site. Those, however, are cases in which the people were already employees and the employers were honest enough to articulate their reasons for firing them. Times that by ten thousand to get the number of times that employers do the same rudimentary research and don't hire a prospective candidate. The only reason they give is, "Thanks for your interest, but your qualifications don't meet our needs at this time."

I have a friend who had been offered a job several years ago when there used to be a popular Web site (since shut down) where you could anonymously post questions or comments about individual employers in that industry. Before my friend accepted the job, he posted a question on this Web site to solicit information about whether this was a good place to work and to get a general idea of what his salary should be. Even though he posted anonymously, the employer rescinded his job offer the next day, saying that he was the only person with an outstanding offer and they were offended by his mentioning their company on that site.

With all the other ways that blacks can draw attention to themselves in ways they have no control over, Internet postings that draw negative attention are something they're in complete control of. (Technically, that's not entirely true since some researchers have found that even photos deleted from a person's social networking site can still turn up in an Internet search later.) It is critical to remember that on the Internet, even when you keep your information private, you have no control over what someone else does with the information, comments, or photos you post. Recently, there was a case where a manager got wind that an employee was doing something a little scandalous on the side. The manager intimidated another employee into accessing the private social networking page of the suspected employee who had earmarked him as a "friend."

Was that an ethical tactic? Hell no. It's even an arguably good case for invasion of privacy, up to a point. But again, we're talking the Internet here. Not breaking into someone's home to read his diary or tap his phones. Not snooping outside a living room window to peer at the nightly happenings of your subordinate. We're talking posting personal business—private page or not—on the WORLD WIDE WEB.

Let's say that you're one of those people who have sufficient privacy concerns to not post anything lewd, scandalous, embarrassing, or offensive on your Web sites, but you still love your Facebook or BlackPlanet or MySpace visits. That's fine, but love the visits on your own time. Most companies legally can and do monitor the Internet traffic of their employees. Just because your employer doesn't tell you about it or you don't see folks getting fired for it left and right doesn't mean that it doesn't happen. It does. And with the increased popularity of these sites, the number of people who will get fired in the upcoming years will sky-rocket.

Also, as a friend of mine noted, you have to be careful of who has "friended" you on some of these sites, since the activities of the people linked to your pages could put you in a bad light. Some might say that it is going too far to attempt to monitor the behavior of your friends. But what I'm talking about is being more concerned about being safe than sorry, since social networking sites just give new avenues for employers and prospective employers to know what birds of a feather you flock with.

Which is another reason why black employees need to be increasingly vigilant about accessing these sites at work. If your employer ever fires you for excessive use of the Internet because you just can't wait to use your own personal handheld device over break or at lunch, the reason will be as "legitimate and nondiscriminatory" as you can get. It won't matter that Susie looks at Facebook occasionally too or that Gordon is always checking his LinkedIn account. A violation is a violation, and most companies are very clear that they own and monitor the Internet traffic on your work computer. At work, when you use work hardware and software to access these sites, there is no "invasion of privacy" leg to stand on.

Just like the clothes you wear to work, the hair you sport, and the conversation you engage in, putting all your business on a social networking site is like waving a red flag in front of a bull (your employer) and daring it to rush you while you wear high-heel shoes. Think, think again, and at the very least, keep it private!

The positive aspect of social networking for blacks—which should be taken better advantage of by those aiming to be drivers of their careers in Corporate America rather than just responders—is that it does offer greater and heightened opportunities to network with others in a way that traditionally could only be accomplished by attending an expensive conference or convention out of town. LinkedIn.com is an especially good Web site for connecting with other professionals concerning all aspects of your career.

More important, in being able to more easily connect with other blacks, social networking offers you not only the opportunity to make great contacts for when you want to change careers but also an opportunity to realize that there may be more people just like you doing the same or even greater things in other companies and organizations. And that kind of exposure to the successes of others can be a great motivator as you walk on your own professional journey.

7

FRIENDS, FOES, AND FAKERS

■

Todd, a black computer software engineer, was home sick for three days. The only time he left his apartment was to see the doctor and go to the pharmacy to get the medicine that his doctor prescribed for him.

Todd was having trouble with his boss, Jessica, a white woman. He was the only black man in his department, and he was fairly sure that his direct, slightly abrasive style of talking clashed routinely with Jessica's gentle, laid-back, Southern-fried charm and mode of speaking. Wayne, an older black supervisor from the human resources department whom Todd only knew in passing, called Todd to his office the day he got back from having been ill. Todd was puzzled because there was no work-related reason for Wayne to talk to him, and they never rolled together socially. When he arrived at Wayne's office, out of the blue Wayne said, "Man, if you're going to lie and call in sick, at least make it look good and stay at home in case someone calls." Todd was stunned.

Apparently Jessica had gone to Wayne to report her suspicion that Todd was faking his illness. Wayne volunteered to call Todd at home to check on her suspicion. The only problem with that scenario was that Wayne happened to call during the two-hour block of time Todd was visiting his doctor and getting his prescription filled—something he figured out when Todd angrily showed him the three bottles of medication his doctor ordered him to take for the next two weeks.

Wayne had told Jessica that Todd probably didn't answer his phone because he was sleeping. He thought he had done Todd a favor.

Although some people are more social than others, the bonds you form at work can be the key not just to your success but also to your contentment. Whether you're a survivor, a striver, or a thriver, it makes the day go easier if the people you have to deal with are people you like and trust.

If you ever watched the television show *Survivor*, where people are stuck on an island and the last one standing wins one million dollars, then you know as the number of people dwindles down, the more the folks on the show love to talk about alliances. It's all a game of keeping track of who seems to be in whose pocket. The fascinating aspect is watching the alliances shift as each person gets closer to that million dollars. In the beginning, while a person's alliance might be to the person who can best catch a fish, it starts getting more about which of the people remaining you think you can beat.

The workplace is a lot like the game of *Survivor*—minus the island, eating bugs for lunch, and having a shot at a million dollars. It is an environment where you have to negotiate personal politics on a daily basis.

Most workers deal with camaraderie issues—whom to befriend, whom to enjoy, and whom to eat lunch with. That's a basic 85 percent issue. A black survivor will be the least concerned with giving thought to her alliances. If the survivor isn't of the loner variety, she will ally with anyone who crosses her path regularly and shows consistent pleasantness.

Strivers, because they are more focused on trying to get ahead, pick allies a bit more strategically. A black striver either is or should be allied with the people who have the biggest potential to take her where she wants to go. It isn't about using people—using people is when you pretend to like people you don't for no other reason than to get some advantage you wouldn't otherwise have. Strategically making friends and allies in the workplace is a matter of getting to know people slowly and from there deciding how a bond between the two of you can work best.

The thrivers—black employees who have their own irrepressible style—make allies similar to the way survivors do. Neither pays a whole lot of attention to picking the "right" people to know or the appropriate people to bond with. In general, thrivers tend to operate from more of a gut-level instinct on whom to hang with at work and whom not to. Once, when doing witness interviews at a company, I talked with a young black man who was close friends with an older white coworker who was known for saying the *n*-word occasionally and making off-color jokes. When I asked the brother why he was so tight with the guy, he simply said, "I like him; he's real." Talking some more with the young man, I found out that he liked his white coworker because he always knew where he stood with the man, and in general, the man had his back. That is definitely a thriver way of looking at workplace friendships.

Alliances in the workplace are not monochromatic. As tempting as it may be, it would be a mistake to enter a new job and decide that all the black people are your friends, all the white people are your enemies, and everyone else should be judged by whether he or she seems to take the side of blacks or whites. This overly simplistic analysis will get you into trouble every time.

Even though I've said that most blacks in the workplace are either survivors, strivers, or thrivers, the reality is that on some level, we are all survivors trying to figure out the optimal way to do our jobs each day. We all want to love the career path we're on and enjoy the rest of our lives when we're not on the clock. Except for a rare chosen few, we don't live to work; we work to live. However, it matters whom we share the bulk of our work-days with—whether they are people we enjoy, trust, and respect, and whether they are people who validate us, or at the very least don't invalidate us.

So how does a black employee pick alliances in the work-place? If you're smart, hopefully you can start before you even begin the job. Picking alliances is the one area of the work experience where being a driver doesn't come into play so much. While you can aim to be smart about whom you trust and whom you align yourself with, you can only be so calculated about making those choices.

I think it was General Patton who said that taking a calculated risk is not the same thing as being rash. However, when it comes to friends and allies in the workplace, you may end up being rash because you can't factor in, and therefore cannot control, the human element—that is, the human element of just hitting it off with some people more than others. Sure, you can try to pick the right people to ally yourself with at work, but your pickings exist without any input from you.

I'd like to think that I'm as close as anyone I know to being a driver when it comes to alliances. I never underestimate the importance of anyone; therefore, my plate of friends and associates at work has always been large. As I said earlier, being a driver is about the conscious choices you make rather than the instinctive ones you make as a survivor, striver, or thriver. If you consciously choose your friends, you are increasing your chances of success at work by making it a better and more trusting place to be.

The reason you choose, whether you're a survivor, striver, or thriver, is that if you stand out, you want to know if you stand alone. It's always dangerous to walk into a work situation assuming who will or won't have your back. I like the old saying "The enemy of my enemy is my friend," because it is a reminder of the importance of knowing how people are connected. This is sometimes the most powerful piece of information you have. When I was a reporter and covered a beat, I learned that the quickest way to find out information was to figure out how it flowed. You figured that out by finding out the real ties that bind. If I know (despite the fact that it isn't public knowledge) that City Councilmember Sue hates the mayor but is best buds with Councilmember Frank, who is super tight with City Planner Marco, the best person to go to for background on possible budget cuts will probably be Councilmember Frank's secretary. Why? Because Frank will know the dirt from hanging out with Sue and the implications from chilling with Marco, and Frank's secretary will usually be the unconnected, accidental witness to what her boss knows. In simpler terms, to keep up with what's affecting your work world, you need to know who has pertinent information and in what direction that information flows. But during your first few days on a new job, there's no way you'll know these subtleties.

Additionally, whether you like it or not, as a black person you directly or indirectly have a relationship with every other black person who works at that place. From day one you will be judged, and for the most part, your harshest critics on the issue of alliances will be your black coworkers. You'll be judged by how you speak to other blacks, which blacks you do and don't speak to, and which blacks you do and don't become friends with. If you become friends or allies with coworkers who aren't black, the trustworthiness of those relationships will be judged by how you relate to your black coworkers.

Black Like Me

We black people are a communal lot. When enough of us get together, even if we're total strangers, we can make any event a prayer meeting, a fight, or a party depending on who, what, when, and where. That's one of the reasons why, when blacks enter a new work situation, we usually do an automatic gut check on what's up with the other blacks who work there—to figure out who to be cool with and who to avoid like the Jheri curl.

In the summer of 2002 I was one of about forty people anxiously waiting in line on the first day to purchase tickets to a Luther Vandross concert. That short forty-five-minute event was a microcosm of how black people get along—you saw shouting, raucous laughter, anger, suspicion, folks cussing over love and money, instant bonding of friends, and the formation of enemies. You saw the whole theater of white people at the ticket booth rolling their eyes, the sister girl brought in from the back to tame the unruly masses, and plain good-spirited unruliness—with just enough order and organization to keep it from breaking out into a straight up fight worthy of calling in the police. By the time the last person in line bought her ticket (while steadily complaining about the cost of the ticket and how far back her seats were), all was right with the world. Strangers became friends, vowing to look for each other at the concert. People who hadn't seen each other in a while caught up on old times and exchanged new numbers. The sister chastised by the group for not saving a place for a stranger who needed to run to the ATM was welcomed back into the fold. And the white ticket sellers looked relieved and surprised it all ended so well. It was loud. It was colorful. It didn't make no damn sense, and yet it moved in perfect order. It was so wonderfully black.

In the workplace, black people work a lot of the theater found in that concert line into our jobs. It's more like a soap opera than a feature film, but the dynamics are the same. I mention the Luther Vandross ticket story as an example of how the energy changes when several black people get together. Except for the most bourgeois of black folks at a black-tie event, when blacks start interacting in groups, we can't help but get boisterous. Even if our voices don't get louder than a whisper, we shake things up when we get together.

What makes the workplace such a soap opera sometimes is that most people crave the sameness and repetitiveness of human events. In foreign environments, especially ones that are somewhat threatening, you look for patterns, sameness, themes, anything that reminds you of territory you've walked before. This is an 85 percent issue—one all workers can relate to.

Workplace Politics

There are certain phrases that always make me cringe whenever I hear them, and I always mentally correct them in my head. In the context of the workplace, one of them is "My job doesn't have workplace politics." Because I have a big mouth, I usually don't just keep my thoughts to myself. I usually say that even if only three people work together, workplace politics kick in whenever one of them leaves the room.

Workplace politics are about alliances, viewpoints, opinions, knowledge, information, power, and how all those things intersect and play off each other. The natural thing for any person to do when he enters a foreign environment is to look for a home. You look for what makes you feel comfortable and safe. You look for the person you can take your cues from. Just like a visitor setting foot in a strange country, no matter how much you've studied the native language, the second you hear an American voice, you don't feel quite so alone.

Because, like everyone else, I like to be comforted in a new environment and I like to get a sense of whom to befriend and from whom to run, my standard mental checklist whenever I start a new job is probably a lot like other black folks'. In no particular order:

- Where's the bathroom?
- Where do I get my coffee?

- Where is my boss's office in relation to mine?
- Where are the other black folks?

I've only had one job where there were no other black employees, and it was no coincidence that it was one of the worst jobs I've ever had.

The assumptions, however, can get you into trouble if you go to work assuming that all other black people operate from the same place you do. I'm sorry to go there, but we all know that some of the most unreasonably stubborn, judgmental people in the history of thinking can be black folks who know what they know, and know how other blacks should behave.

In the example at the beginning of the chapter, Todd was dealing with an age-old truism of working while black—the HNIC. Although many will be offended by my not sanitizing the term, Wayne was the company's Head Nigger in Charge. It's a concept as widespread and well known as crabs in the barrel. You know that syndrome? Where one black climbs up the ladder of success (a crab) and his fellow black coworkers (the other crabs) scramble like crazy to bring him back down into the barrell with the rest of them? God forbid one of them gets out if the rest of them can't all get out at the same time. It seems to me that the HNIC is the crab at the top of the barrel policing the rim to kick the other crabs right back to the bottom. Or at least trying to, anyway.

In the example given, Wayne wasn't being nothing more than an HNIC. The second Jessica came to him with some bullcrap about not believing that Todd was really out sick, instead of playing "I Spy," Wayne should have merely told Jessica to request medical documentation from Todd when he returned. Even then she should only do that if it were her policy with every other employee in her department who was out sick for more than a day or two. Otherwise, Wayne is just participating in the workplace version of black-on-black crime. What does an HNIC gain at work for taking such action? It's today's spin on being a "house nigger" versus being a field slave—a black or a set of blacks always strive for the "in" slot with the whites in charge at the expense of other blacks.

The HNIC is usually the first black still around to have worked with the employer. Other times it's the black employee who makes the most money or has the highest title. In some ways, HNICs are probably less prevalent in the workplace today than they were twenty or thirty years ago when there were more real "firsts."

When you suspect a person you work with may be an HNIC, the best way to deal with her is like the elderly aunt in your family whom you don't really like but whom you go out of your way to be nice to on holidays—you keep the HNIC at bay by showing deference and respect. You do that because often all she wants is an acknowledgment from the young bloods that she exists and that, in some ways, she paved the way. The good thing about paying that respect, even if you're secretly rolling your eyes, is that you learn something. Like with the old aunt, you learn some history, some background, and maybe even some genuine advice that helps make your experience easier. Any black person who has survived in a workplace for a period of time deserves our respect.

That leads to the next point, which is making sure that you don't walk in the door making assumptions based on how someone dresses or talks. While there are some people who make better allies than others, all of your fellow employees, particularly the other black ones, deserve a chance to show what they're made of before you jump to conclusions.

When Your Boss Is Black but Not an HNIC

The beautiful thing about more blacks entering the workforce is that the more who do, the more end up filling the ranks of management. It's important to reiterate that not every black in the workplace with a position of authority is an HNIC and, more important, that black employees need to be more deliberate in the ways we treat the black managers and leaders in our workplace.

Many blacks can have very fixed and inflexible judgments about how we believe other blacks are supposed to act in certain situations. For example, many believe that once a black person gets to a high position, she has a responsibility to help the other blacks who come behind her. Any person who has that opinion will defend quite strongly its rightness based along the lines of "They wouldn't have gotten where they are if people hadn't fought for them," "They owe it to the next generation," "White folks look out for each other so we blacks should do the same," and so on.

The problem with all those assessments is that black managers can never win. If they reach out to help other blacks in the company, some will say they aren't doing enough. If they do public work for the black community, then people accuse them of just trying to impress their white bosses. If they merely focus on doing stellar work but don't spend some minimal amount of time rubbing elbows with the "little people," they will be called uppity.

At the end of the day, we as black people need to cut our brothers and sisters who go far at work some slack. They had to work hard to get there, and they oftentimes are balancing every stressor you have as a black person plus some. For example, if you're the assistant to a black executive, stop to think about the fact that how that executive treats you will be under a different kind of scrutiny than if that executive had a white assistant. People will watch to see if the executive is showing you favoritism, bending the rules for you, tolerating sloppier work, or overlooking issues with you that he or she would not overlook with an assistant who wasn't also black. In other words, some people will make sure that two blacks aren't getting over in the company for the price of one.

So as a black person on a lower end of the food chain than your fellow brother or sister, here are some tips that will help you in that situation:

- Unless you truly have a personal relationship that transcends time, space, and paycheck, don't go to a black in the company expecting him or her to run interference on a work problem you are having that has nothing to do with his or her job. The major exception is if you choose to go to a black person in your human resources department to report a complaint involving race because you feel more comfortable doing so.

- If you have a black superior who has a friendly personality and goes the extra bit to be a little warmer to you as a fellow black person, be particularly vigilant in not treating that person any differently at work, especially in front of other people, compared to how you treat his or her white peers. For example, don't call the person by his or her first name if you address everyone else by last name. And, for goodness' sake, no matter how cool you feel with the person, don't fall into personal, casual references like, "What's up, my brotha?" or "Talk to you later, girlfriend."

■ Even if you do all the right things in public, lower your internal expectations. The expectations that blacks have of other blacks can cause unnecessary resentment, not just internally but also to the people you talk to. Having conversations or making comments like "Why doesn't she do more to make sure more blacks are hired?" or "He knows the blacks in this department aren't getting the promotions they should be getting. He's just being a tool of Da Man!" really aren't fair. First, it presumes that any individual has an obligation to take on advocacy because of a status he or she gave no consent to having—in this case race. Second, it also presumes that you have the slightest idea what someone does to promote the same issues you have when you're not privy to the person's actions. For all you know, behind closed doors in management meetings or in committees that you don't even know exist, individual folks with nice titles and even nicer paychecks might be taking stands that would surprise and impress you if brought to light. But one of the reasons why they do have the titles and positions they have is because they play the game differently than you do.

■ And even if they don't play the game at all, if they are doing their jobs well they're still benefiting every black person in the workplace by thumping stereotypes, contradicting negative assumptions, and making it that much harder for folks who don't like blacks in leadership positions to have an example supporting their point.

Workplace Alliances

Marlena worked in a large Fortune 500 company as an auditor. An attractive black woman in her early thirties, she had
worked at the company about five years when Crystal,
another attractive sister, started working as an auditor fresh
out of college. Crystal was very excited about her first job—
a striver for sure.

Marlena (who was also a striver) worked from the
assumption that since she was the "old head," the black person who had gotten to the company first and knew the ins
and outs, Crystal should come up to Marlena first, introduce
herself, pay the requisite respect, and ask Marlena for her
hard-fought wisdom. That's the way Marlena was brought
up by her parents, and she learned in church that you honor
your elders, even if they are only about eight years older.
Marlena thought Crystal was stuck up and wasn't about to
make the first overture.

Crystal, on the other hand, had a different philosophy.
She thought that when she came into a new job it was the
elder's responsibility to welcome her, volunteer her knowledge, and make her path smoother, just as she planned to do
for the brothers and sisters who came after her. Crystal
thought Marlena was a snob.

For over a year, Marlena shrugged Crystal off like a bad
habit while Crystal threw salt Marlena's way every chance
she could. Each of them had built up such an attitude about
the other in her own mind that one wouldn't so much as loan

the other a subway token. The only reason they ever got to know each other and eventually ended up as friends was because Teresa, another young black woman hired a year after Crystal, made it her business to get to know every other black person in her department when she started. Eventually she let both Marlena and Crystal know that the other was a good, trustworthy person and that their snobby sister routines were only helping their supervisor to pit them against each other and screw them both over.

Alliances are probably the most complex aspect of working. A friend of mine who has a job as a supervisor once called me complaining about how much people talk about non-work-related topics in the workplace. I pointed out to her that running your mouth at work was the social lubricant that kept the wheels of employment turning. She had to be reminded that her utter lack of socializing in past jobs was why she was the last to know about impending layoffs that affected her department and about upcoming key personnel changes that ended up causing her problems because she knew later rather than sooner. She eventually understood that while doing her job was her number-one objective, it wouldn't kill her to spend five minutes here and there tripping over the company grapevine.

Whether you're a survivor, a striver, or a thriver, the game plan is the same—you have to go in remembering that you are not an island. It's corny but true. It doesn't matter if you're too shy to mutter a hello. You can't miss an opportunity to forge a valuable alliance at work. It's not about using people, it's about allowing yourself to make your work experience as positive as you can. Ultimately, that is what you have to do as a black employee—create and build alliances, not expect them to already exist.

One of the first things you should do when you look for workplace alliances is view and evaluate the coworkers who do the job you are hired to do. If you are a secretary, get to know the other secretaries in your office—don't be so hung up on race that you fail to see that the person whom you can have the best rapport with is a white person old enough to be your mother or a Hispanic person young enough to be your son. Bonding with another employee who does the same job doesn't mean you have to divulge your salary or share your personal secrets. It just means that you resist the tendency to pigeonhole people on first sight and make the assumption that you couldn't possibly have something in common with someone who is a different race, a different sexual orientation, the opposite sex, or significantly older or younger than you.

Part of the difficulty in forming workplace alliances is that people have so many other considerations to juggle that it makes it hard to determine whom to trust, how far that trust should go, and how everyone else might perceive a particular alliance. As I said earlier, having an "old head," a person you can rely on in the workplace, can be helpful in making sure you attract and maintain healthy alliances. Ideally, all your workplace associates and friends can serve as mentors, each in his or her own way.

Challenging Friendships in the Workplace

Wendy, a black assembly-line worker, became good friends with Scott, a white assembly-line worker. They shared a love of old Western movies and Mexican food, and they were both from small towns. Wendy was happily married and was friends with many of the other black assembly-line workers, but because Scott was not only a man but a white one at that, Wendy dealt with her share of people making snide comments about her *boyfriend* or references to *The Odd Couple*.

Wendy, however, wasn't going to let other people's opinions bother her. Scott was the only person who would take overtime shifts for her when she needed to take care of her sick child, and he covered for her when their supervisor asked about a problem she had while working a certain piece of equipment. They shared nothing more than simple friendship. Scott had her back, period, as much as some of her black coworkers and more than others.

Wendy had to face the fact that interracial relationships in the workplace, particularly with a member of the opposite sex, just draw more attention.

How does a black person handle opposite-sex friendships in the workplace? Although that is a tricky area in one respect (with so much talk about sexual harassment), it really should not be handled much differently than making any other alliance.

It starts with not making assumptions about who people are. As a new employee or an employee trying to get to know a new employee, you should consider professional courtesy and friendliness good things. Without jumping too quickly into shop talk or overly personal talk, let people reveal who they are. As I've said throughout this chapter, just listening without preconceived ideas will help you out more than anything.

When it comes to sexual innuendo, that's always out. Period. Regardless of the person's race, his or her position, or how cool he or she seems with it, just keep the sexual jokes out of the workplace. If you do that, nobody will ever be able to say that a relationship with a coworker, let alone a subordinate or a boss, is out of line. These days, even compliments about someone's hair or clothes can have you wading into dangerous territory if you don't know the person really well.

This advice applies to women as well as men. When women start making too many jokes of a sexual nature, it's hard for a man to know when he has crossed the line when he makes one himself. Also, if a woman ever wants to make a complaint about offensive behavior or comments of a sexual nature, the last thing she needs is to have her employer show that she too is a dirty bird. One of the elements that courts look at in deciding whether a hostile sexual work environment exists is "welcomeness," which is if the accuser behaved in a way that might have signaled she was not offended.

With men and women working side by side, I don't think making friendships with people of the opposite sex holds the same problems that it used to; but where it can be a 15 percent issue for a black employee is a situation in which a white employee who is not used to dealing with blacks socially takes friendliness to be something more. Even in today's society, black men cannot afford to be in positions in which their actions look sexual or predatory in nature around white women. Black men and white women can be friends at work—and plenty are—but black men should not take for granted that their friendships won't offend someone at work if they don't read the smoke signals properly.

In addition to avoiding anything sexual, black employees should be very observant about the ways the rest of their coworkers do certain things and follow those leads. For example, if you work in a place where everyone goes out to lunch in groups rather than in pairs, you will draw attention if you and an opposite-sex coworker always go out to lunch together. Even if nothing is going on, you risk the appearance that it is, or you risk your coworker taking your behavior the wrong way with no one else around to back you up. Granted, that can still happen if you work in a place where employees go to lunch in pairs, but it draws less attention if you're just rolling with the norm.

Alliances Between Black Men and Black Women

Roland was a black college student who had a summer internship in a predominantly white office. Another black intern, Lisa, had developed a dislike for Roland by the end of the summer because he never went to lunch with her even though he went to lunch with the other (white male) interns. Later, when they were both hired, she found out from talking to another person in the office that Roland didn't go to lunch with women, period, because he was afraid of someone assuming that he was interested in them romantically or sexually.

While Roland's instincts as an intern not wanting to make any false steps may have been sound, his execution of this intent was greatly flawed. With the exception of some fields like construction work or nursing where there is a disproportionate number of people of one sex doing the job, you are going to have to deal fairly equally with members of the opposite sex. Avoidance is not a good tactic. In Roland's case, he had a lot in common with Lisa just by the two of them being the only black interns in a big company. While that did not mean they would necessarily bond, Roland never got the opportunity to know because he took the path of least resistance and left the door closed.

Hierarchical Relationships Between Black Employees

Another tricky aspect of building alliances is bonding with your black supervisor or subordinate. A lot of times the person with whom you have the most in common is another brother or sister who is your boss or whom you are the boss of. It can be done if the two of you keep your personal relationship out of the workplace. One way you do that is by keeping those alliances to a minimum and keeping work out of personal conversations as much as possible when you do hang out. Also, do not rub in your personal relationship with others at work, because that will just cause undue resentment from the white people who will question your objectivity.

Blacks and Formalized Unions

For some, unions are the one-size-fits-all way of choosing alliances. The existence of unions isn't as prevalent as it used to be, but in theory they have the right idea. People bond over the common tie of doing the same job or sharing the same craft, and they vow to stand together and protect each other's interests.

If you are a black person in the union, don't be a passive participant. Do more than pay your union dues—go to meetings, read the newsletter, run for office if you're a striver, and be a union steward if you're a thriver. Find whatever way works best for you to be active and involved so that your official brotherhood means something.

This advice—about being an active participant in widening your workplace alliances—holds true even if you do not belong to a union. If there are committees or task forces in your workplace, join them. Don't be afraid, intimidated, or just plain disinterested because it appears that only the white employees get involved. My grandmother gave me that piece of advice a long time ago in the context of shopping, and it holds even more true in the workplace—wherever you see all the white people going, that's where you want to at least visit to see what you may be missing.

Blacks and the Gay and Lesbian Community

In the last few years, I have facilitated and led dozens of workplace diversity workshops and events. One of the disturbing trends I've noticed is for black and Hispanic employees to openly make offensive and disparaging remarks about gay people. And worse, when the individuals who do so get called on it, they defend their right to be rude.

At one workshop, there were about twenty people from the company attending, and one of the black women made several offensive remarks about the gay community. I stopped her by saying, "Do you know that depending on what statistics you go by, there is a good chance that at least four people in the room are gay, lesbian, bisexual, or transgender? In fact, since you don't know me, I could be." The woman immediately said, "You're gay?" I replied that I was not but that I could be, as could be several people in the room she didn't know. I also said that if she didn't want folks openly talking about black folks in her presence, she ought to exhibit that same sense of respect for other people.

That particular exchange reminded me of the chasm between people of color and the gay, lesbian, bisexual, and transgender (GLBT) community. Yeah, people like to say that it's mostly about religion, with people of color being more likely to have religious objections to the gay "lifestyle" than whites. I think that's a cop-out. Don't get me wrong, I think the reasons are complex. I think part of the problem is the perception that the GLBT community is dominated by a lot of white people with money who appear to already have plenty of advantages. For blacks in particular, I think part of the problem is the perception that the GLBT community wants to achieve all the rights that blacks had to fight a lot longer for, a lot harder for, and at the expense of a much higher body count. I've even heard blacks who are gay express this very point.

But in the workplace, I think the real issue is that while many gay people are openly and proudly out, many are not. At the very least, in a forum such as a diversity workshop, you can't look around the room and decide which strangers are gay or not. Sure, a lot of people think they can rely on stereotypes to figure out who is gay, but they can't. Therefore, it becomes easy to talk about folks who aren't there. Only they *are* there.

It reminds me of when people say, "I don't know anyone who is gay." I always say, "Yeah, you do. You just don't know it." And what this has to do with blacks getting along in the workplace is this: everyone who has experienced discrimination in any form, whether it's discrimination you "agree" with or not, is a potential ally. If someone understands what it is like to be treated poorly because of who he or she is, then respect that person if nothing else.

One of the places where we saw "competing" bigotry take place was in California in 2008 when the GLBT community, in throwing its collective support to the election of the first black presidential nominee in a major party, got upset that a large number of black voters did not support voting for the legalization of gay marriage. This was quite controversial, but where you sit or stand on the issue is less important than realizing that this was an example of the growing chasm between the GLBT community and the black community. I don't think it can ever fully be resolved in the political arena—there are too many complicated issues that will continue to rub against each other—but in the workplace, it just doesn't pay to gay bash.

To be a driver in the workplace (instead of instinctively operating from one of the survivor, striver, or thriver mind-sets), it is important to honor the individuality of people no matter who they are. Developing workplace alliances isn't about using people; it's about thoughtfully befriending them for the purpose of making your work experience smoother and more positive. Part of thoughtfully befriending is not to instinctively classify an individual based on race, sex, sexuality, or any other category. Otherwise you may miss seeing who really has your back and who is admiring the surface of your back for the knife he'll eventually stick in it. Especially when you're in a new environment, the best advice for sifting out alliances is just to lean back, listen, and learn.

8

FITTING IN WHILE STANDING OUT, SETTLING IN WITHOUT SELLING OUT

■

Frank, a black marketing analyst, didn't believe in attending company parties. He adamantly refused to go to any social event that did not take place during his normal work hours. He had a wife, four school-age children, and aging parents with health problems; he was active in his church and college fraternity; and he was an avid bowler.

As long as he gave a hundred percent to his job, which he did when he was there, Frank didn't think it mattered or should matter whether he broke bread or hoisted a beer with his coworkers after work every now and then or attended the company-sponsored get-togethers. He thought those parties were for people trying to kiss ass or people who didn't have a real life like he did. He also harbored the bias passed down from his parents that it was never a good idea to give white folks an opportunity to see him drink liquor or get too cozy with him.

There is an old deodorant commercial that says that you don't get a second chance to make a first impression. In the workplace, especially when you're black, everything is an impression. Everything. You know it. I know it. Your bosses know it, even though they'll never admit it. First and foremost, though, you always have to keep your eye on the ball. You can spend days on end concerned about how white people perceive you, but you'll only drive yourself crazy.

Part of fitting in means doing your job well. Period. Never slip up on the obvious. If the posted, expressed time for you to be there is 7 A.M., then 7:30 is not an option. If you can't get up that early, then find another job. At most jobs in America, your 7:30 is going to mysteriously be remembered as getting in an hour late every day, while your white coworker who sashays in at 7:10 is going to be remembered as being mostly punctual. Depending on where you work, your coming in even at 7:10 will be examined because of the assumption that the white employee has a good reason, rather than being equally as derelict as yourself. It's just an offshoot of what black parents have told their children about having to get up earlier in the morning to compete. Today's black parents should just tell their kids to get their butts up earlier to at least get to work on time.

In theory, Frank from the example has a point. If you're paid to do a job, why should it matter whether you attend a holiday party, go to a summer picnic, or even have a drink after work with your coworkers? Logically, it makes no sense that additional time away from your family or your own interests should be required if you already give a lot to your job.

This is where knowing your workplace mentality comes in. If you're in it to win it—that is, if you're a striver—it should be a no-brainer that showing up at all company events, unless you have an incredibly good reason, is a must. (Actually, I think it is a must for all black employees, but your mode of operation will just determine how you do it.) Depending on the person and the job, showing up could be a quick visit, a leisurely meet-and-greet opportunity, or an in-your-face chance to show them what you're really made of.

In a nutshell, the reason we need to show up is so that we can demystify ourselves and be revealed as having the same red blood as every other human being on earth. It's an example of how we have to show the people we work with that 85 percent factor, where we are united in our motivation to come to work for the same reasons, regardless of race.

I never cease to be amazed at how unaware many whites are about the diversity among black people. I once took a white coworker to the black neighborhood where I grew up. She was astounded at how "normal" the people were dressed, since she had assumed that the neighborhood folks would resemble something you would see on an old episode of *Starsky and Hutch*. (As I said in an earlier chapter, the blacks that many whites work with are actually their only contact with our world outside of what they see on television or in movies.)

On the other hand, it doesn't really matter what a fellow employee thinks of you, unless you think he is actually trying to do you harm. But managing workplace politics requires you to be as concerned about benign neglect or reckless disregard as much as you should be concerned about active, direct, backstabbing malice.

Be a Driver in the Workplace

The concept of fitting in is practically synonymous with the concept of being a driver. That is, if you are a driver, then you make a conscious choice to fit in when you enter a particular workplace.

Just because you're a black employee does not mean you are going to have trouble fitting in to a predominantly white workplace. Because of your personality or the nature of the job you do, fitting in may be second nature. But when you walk into a new work situation or the old one changes, the realization that you may need to do some adjusting to stay afloat is nothing more than pure driver mentality talking.

Instinctively, no one feels like she should have to change who she is. By choosing to be a driver, you're simply acknowledging that you are allowing yourself to shine in your best light. You're deciding to keep certain conversations out of the workplace. You're making the choice to keep certain interests to yourself. It's not about change; it's about making adjustments to reach your goal. A survivor's goal may be just not to draw undue attention.

A striver's goal may be to draw the attention of the right bosses. A thriver's goal may be not to stand out so much that it prevents him from doing his job properly.

So what does this have to do with attending company parties and socializing with your coworkers? Easy: it's much harder to do harm to or create a bad experience for a friend than for a stranger. Overall, white people tend to think of friends in a much broader, more superficial spectrum than blacks. Black people have always used language to reflect our rich, ceaseless devotion to how we define and are connected to others in our life. A white person will typically refer to his *friend*, *pal*, or *buddy*. A black person, on the other hand, will talk about his *blood*, *homey*, *ace*, *brother* or *sister*, *partner*, *cousin*, *my M.F.*, *my n*****, and so on. Not only will we use variety in our names, we will be quick to correct others on the distinctions. "Frank is my running buddy, but Mike is my ace." "Teresa is my girl, but Carrie is like my sister."

I think blacks as a communal group are clear about who knows our secrets, who knows our lies, and who knows nothing more than how much ice we like in our drinks. No matter what generation of blacks you look to, we've always had a thing about folks knowing our business. A long time ago, the black comic Marsha Warfield (who played the role of Roz the bailiff on *Night Court*), said black people couldn't play the game Trivial Pursuit because we only have three possible answers to every question, and one is "Why you wanna know?"

Even our collective struggle as blacks and how we refer to ourselves—*colored* versus *black* versus *African American*—gets to our bottom-line issue of defining our relationship to other people. It's like the Yoruba proverb that says, "It's not what I'm called, it's what I answer to." But the truth is, it does matter what we're called. As author Toni Morrison said, "American means white, and Africanist people struggle to make the term applicable to themselves with ethnicity and hyphen after hyphen after hyphen."

If you can get a white coworker to call you "friend" at work, it's a lot more likely that the person will pause before stabbing you in the back. It also makes it more likely that the person will be your ally and a true comrade in the workplace. At the very least, your proximity might make you more alert to the presence of hot metal approaching your back. All whites are not your enemy, but to the extent some are, as the saying goes, keep your friends close and your enemies closer. Or, as Oprah Winfrey has said, "Surround yourself only with people who are going to lift you higher."

Accepting someone as an individual, without stereotyping, is the first step toward becoming his or her friend. If I think of you as someone who can be hurt by what I do or say, I'm going to be a lot less likely to make you an object of my harmful actions. Maybe it's just me, but if I think of someone as a friend, I'll guard his interests with almost as much care as I guard my own. On the other hand, if I don't think of someone as a friend, either because I actively dislike him or just don't consider him in my universe at all, then I'm indifferent about my words or actions where that person is concerned. I treasure my friends in the workplace. I don't expect them to scratch my back, I just expect them to let me know if there is a "Kick Me" sign taped to it.

From a practical standpoint, when someone files a discrimination lawsuit, one thing that happens is the defense attorneys investigate and talk to everyone who worked with the plaintiff to see what's up. The more friends you have, the more people you will have to support your interpretation of the events. (Never underestimate how a little loyalty will go a long way in that situation.)

Part of our reality as black employees is that we operate against the backdrop of a collective stereotype. That is, if you're black, you came from a poor, lower-class home without a father or positive male role model in which you were exposed to drugs, poverty, excessive use of alcohol, and sex. You weren't exposed to the "nicer" things in life. That's the presumption until we say differently.

When you go to company picnics and holiday parties, bringing your husband, wife, significant other, relative, or friend, it is a way to make your experience as a black person count in a world where it just doesn't pay to be a statistic. It's one thing to know that Rufus is married. It's another thing to know that his wife's name is Susan and she seems mighty sweet and likes to cook pound cake and whatever other details about his life that make Rufus a person to whom it's easier to relate. While you don't want to parade your straight-up dirt in the workplace, don't be afraid to sneak in enough of your outside life to show you as more than an ignorable black face.

In Frank's example from the beginning of this chapter, the one thing that Frank did do to personalize himself and thus make him more approachable in the eyes of his coworkers and superiors was to openly talk about his children and family. He brought in pictures, displayed his kids' artwork in his cubicle, and occasionally brought the children into work for brief visits. That in part made up for Frank's failure to show up at company-sponsored events. And that's why, when one of Frank's children came down with a serious illness, his company didn't hesitate to let him off for a few weeks with pay, send his family a huge fruit basket, and make it easy for him when he came back to work. Considering that his company was too small to be covered by the Family and Medical Leave Act (FMLA), that was a generous gesture on his employer's part. (The FMLA federally mandates that companies of a certain size offer a leave of absence to employees who have personal health problems or close relatives with health problems. In addition to other conditions, such as the length of time allowed, the leave is not required to be paid. The point of the leave is to allow a person to have a job to come back to if he or she has a personal or family health problem.)

My guess is that if Frank's white supervisors had not consistently seen how much fatherhood mattered to Frank, he would have been left taking time off for his child with no pay and having to worry about job security while he was gone. In some workplaces, he wouldn't have had the option of taking any time at all, because the assumption would have been that he was just trying to get a few extra days off.

Allowing your bosses to peek into your personal reality is no magic bullet against a truly racist boss. Handled carelessly, too much information (known by the younger set as "TMI") can be used as a weapon against you. It takes constantly evolving judgment to know what to share and what to keep on the down low. For example, telling your bosses that you are stressed because of a close relative's health problem is probably a good thing. Telling them you can't decide whether to put yourself in rehab or just to try cutting back to four benders a week is something you might want to keep to yourself. Sharing with your bosses that you're going through a painful divorce might be a good thing. Telling them how you just caught your boyfriend in bed with your best friend the night before—which is why you were two hours late for work after needing to be bailed out of jail—is probably something you should keep to yourself. I think the trick to good judgment should be keeping your professionalism at the forefront of what you decide to share.

The best combination is to concentrate on doing a good job first and then sharing information about yourself that shows you are also a good person and that sometimes your life as an employee can be influenced by your life outside of work. This is particularly true with your coworkers as well as your supervisors. Letting them know that you have a thing for NASCAR, that you like to play tennis on the weekends, or that you are planning on taking piano lessons makes it a little easier to fit in while staying true to yourself.

Deciding How Many of Your True Colors to Show

There are subtle ways that, as a black employee, you can be known and develop a more well-rounded relationship with your workplace. One of these is how you choose to show off in your environment. With the exception of people who work in factories or out in the field (such as sales representatives), most employees have a workstation, a cubicle, or an office to call their own at the place where they make their weekly bread. Every form of decoration or addition of detail tells your coworkers and your employer about your life and your interests, providing a peek into who you really are.

Again, part of letting yourself be known is just giving yourself an entry point for others—a place where you can meet at the common ground of 85 percent experiences. My point is not to make your environment white or white centered, it's to make your environment right for you. For example, if you love baseball but your hero is Buck O'Neil from the Kansas City Monarchs, a Negro League team, put up his poster or display his autographed baseball, regardless of whether you're a survivor, a striver, or a thriver. This might give a white colleague who shares your interest in baseball the opportunity to connect with you while learning something. On the other hand, a white colleague might surprise you by sharing your love of Buck O'Neil, thus giving you another ally in the workplace.

A friend of mine frequently complains about how he hates always having to "teach" white people—that we have to constantly expose them to more about our world while we are expected to soak up every nuance of theirs. He's right. I get tired, too. The thing about other ethnic groups that we might not necessarily know much about, either, is that there is no expectation that we should know. For example, it's not expected to know about Chinese New Year or Cinco de Mayo, but we better know about St. Patrick's Day.

With whites at work, it's supposed to be a given that we know all. The unspoken theme is: if it interests white America, it's interesting. But that's the price tag on choosing to interact in a space where people who look like me are not the ones running things. Sometimes I remind myself that the teaching comes from the doing, not the saying, anyway. (Remember, the proof is in the pudding, not the pudding mix.) Besides, as black Americans, we can sometimes arrogantly think we are the only ones with things to teach. One of my favorite foods is sushi. I learned to love it in the early 1990s when another reporter, a white guy originally from Seattle, invited me to lunch at a Japanese restaurant. The two of us may have lost touch, but my love for sushi remained.

When I needed to learn about Alzheimer's disease recently, a white woman attorney (and true friend) passed on information about nursing homes and other places where I could find out more. Along the way, many of my white coworkers, as well as white subordinates and supervisors, have shared all kinds of information, support, and knowledge when I've needed it, as well as when I didn't know I needed it.

The real point here is that opening up the door in the first place allows it to then swing both ways. If I hang up a print by Jacob Lawrence in my office because I really like his art, a couple of my coworkers may develop an appreciation for his work. That's more important in the long run than the people who discount any art that is not white and European in origin. Building support and enough connection with people to stay in the loop is the true point.

A survivor's objective in the workplace when it comes to fitting in will be to avoid standing out as much as possible. Therefore, a survivor should and will go to all the company social events, express interest in the things that coworkers bring to her, and keep her personal life or viewpoints to a minimum for fear that something will be used against her. In terms of decoration, a survivor will stick to the safe things—plants, an old black-and-white wedding photo of her parents, a banner from her college, or a sporting souvenir from the local team. A survivor's goal in decoration is to have people feel comfortable when they are in the survivor's workspace but not have anything excessively memorable.

On the other hand, a striver's objective will be very pinpointed and deliberate. A striver should figure out exactly what she is striving for and whom in particular she needs to impress.

If there is a particular position she wants, she has to remember that it is important for more than just the person in charge of giving the job to like her. She would be wise to attract the good graces of everyone who is affected by her getting that job. For example, if you work in an environment where people like to talk about the latest movies, bringing in some of your film memorabilia from home is a good idea. On the other hand, if you work in an environment filled with regular churchgoers and the person handing out the promotion you want is a deacon of his congregation, you might want to keep that picture of you from the Wiccan induction ceremony at home.

A thriver has just as much reason to attend the company gatherings and pay attention to what his environment reflects as the survivor and the striver do. While marching to his own drumbeat, the thriver still needs to figure out what the rest of the band is doing. Individuality is a thing of sparkling beauty, but unless you're a self-employed entrepreneur with no employees other than yourself, you've got to get into the rhythm of what others are thinking at the place where you collect that cash.

Black people know that the sister-girl receptionist sitting by the elevator has the power to affect whether you'll see the official power behind the golden doors. We also know that the brother-man custodian who cleans offices every night has the power to make sure that the private document that should have been shredded will accidentally make its way into your in-box. Again, that is why it is important to know your intention so that you are aware of all the players in the drama, not just the ones you think have lead roles.

Feeling in tune with the rhythm of your workplace means that you get along with people to make your work life as stress free as you can, your home life as protected as you can, and your opportunity to move on to another gig as painless and easy as possible. As Ida B. Wells said, "Let the Afro-American depend on no party, but on himself, for his salvation. Let him continue toward education, character, and above all, put money in his purse."

I frequently wonder if we black people who have to work almost daily in the white work world are bilingual or just plain schizophrenic. One of the things I love about driving to work in the morning is that often it's the last contact I have with being submerged in my culture until the end of the day. I love listening to the radio and hearing the DJs joke about the latest thing our people are talking about. I look forward to hearing the latest jam from a soul singer before having to submerge myself into a world that's more about Shania Twain or Miley Cyrus.

Like a Hispanic who speaks Spanish at home but doesn't mutter so much as a *gracias* while at work, we black people often feel like we're stepping in and out of parallel worlds. That's why many white bosses get a little nervous when they see more than two of us talking at work—usually our body language, our tone, our laughter reflect that we're dipping back into our comfort zone for a couple of minutes and that they are the ones who are irrelevant. They don't like that feeling.

Being true to your authentic self is the single most important thing you take into each experience. Work is no exception. In general, the concept of fitting in is not about squeezing yourself into a neat little two-dimensional screen that makes others feel more comfortable with you.

Ideally, if you've followed the other guidelines in the earlier part of the book, fitting into the place you work is a natural thing. That's because, if you've identified what motivates you and makes you happy and you've found a career or job that fulfills that goal, then you've already done your research to find the right employer in that field. Form good alliances once you get there, because fitting in is much smoother than being the outsider.

On the other hand, if done right, the flow can follow you. The people in my former law firm, from the managing partner to the file clerk, probably didn't quite picture an attorney in the package of a dreadlock-wearing black woman who keeps crystals on her desk, seriously refers to people's astrological charts, and is comfortable with voicing the off-color comment that most people have enough sense to keep in their heads. But I'd like to think that I did fit in to the point of being missed when I left the firm, because most of who I am makes me a normal 85 percenter just like every other employee, with the rest being my particular brand of flavor.

9

WHEN ATTITUDE IS THE ISSUE

■

Shanice's first annual evaluation was due. Patrick, her supervisor, told her that he wanted her to do a written self-evaluation and turn it in to him before she received his evaluation. Shanice had not been given the criteria she was to be judged by, and she had never received a written set of goals to meet. All she received was a generic list of ratings ranging from one (unacceptable) to five (outstanding), so Shanice took a copy of her job description and wrote a point-by-point analysis of how she felt she had done her job that year. Shanice fairly and objectively, in her mind, ranked herself as either a four or five in each area, giving examples but also listing ways she felt she could improve.

During the next staff meeting after she had turned in her self-evaluation, Patrick remarked to Shanice, in front of sev-

eral of her coworkers, "You think pretty highly of yourself,
don't you?" When Shanice sat down for her evaluation, he
told her, "I haven't done your evaluation yet. I thought I'd
give you an opportunity to redo yours before I did that."

This chapter begins our departure from focusing mostly on the
85 percent issues to issues where the 15 percent difference kicks
in ferociously. This chapter addresses the "attitude" problem, also
known as coming to work black. Since that sounds so negative,
I have to explain it.

First of all, part of the problem with telling people that they
have an attitude problem is that it is a subjective call. What you
call "attitude" I might call "righteous indignation." What you
call "attitude" I might call "frustration." What you call "attitude" I might call "personality." While the interpretation of an
attitude is subjective, when used in the hands of your employer,
the issue of an employee's attitude is a mighty powerful tool.
Saying that an employee has an attitude problem is one of those
blanket terms just about everything can fall under. If you're late
for work a couple of times a week, no matter how many times
your supervisor scolds you, then you might be pegged with an
attitude problem. If you roll your eyes every time your boss mentions the company retreat, you might be perceived as having an
attitude problem. If you never volunteer for new projects while
little Peggy Sue always sticks her hand up, you might be tagged
with an attitude problem.

Every time your boss sticks that label on you, it's not necessarily wrong. Some people do have generally funky attitudes. You

know them. So do I. They have a smart-ass answer for everything, are unnecessarily argumentative, or have one relationship
problem after another without appearing to learn any lessons.
Where attitude becomes an issue for a black person in the workplace, however, is when a black employee does not feel that his
employer is doing right by him and suspects it is because he is
black, or at least suspects that it is based on some reason that is
not fair. Before that employee gets to the point of filing a complaint, he usually develops an "attitude" to carry him through
this rough work environment.

Ironically, my observation has been that it is usually the survivors and the strivers who develop attitudes when they perceive
unfairness in the workplace. You see, I believe that thrivers have
built-in "attitudes" throughout their work experience, which
doesn't drastically change when they perceive a problem. It is survivors (who feel like they are just minding their own business)
and strivers (who have been focused on advancement) who get
thrown for a loop when things are not as they think they should
be. Because neither of those personality types tend to buck the
system anyway, they are more likely to demonstrate an "attitude"
when they perceive anything smelly in the air.

Fighting a bad attitude and maintaining a good one can be
the single most challenging area of your work life as a driver.
When the situation starts to go sour either because of the 85 percent issues that every one of your coworkers would complain
about or the 15 percent issues of "It's a black thang and you
wouldn't understand," it becomes hard to drive yourself from
underneath the covers without copping an attitude. When you
feel the attitude creeping into your system or you know your
anger and resentment are being perceived as attitude by your
employer, that is when you have to become a driver. That is when

you have to consciously snatch yourself by the back of the neck, figure out what's going on, and come up with a game plan for how you're going to lick it. If you need to ask for a transfer, do it. If you need to start sending out resumes, do it. If you need to talk to someone you trust at your workplace who has the power to change things and who you don't think will burn you, do it.

When attitude becomes the issue for you as a black person, you've got to take action. Sometimes that action is with yourself, and sometimes it's with someone else. Sometimes the action is just to get the hell out of there.

One of the ways a black employee can guard against having an attitude that becomes a work problem is to accept that no matter how you work and how good you are, you may run across someone who feels differently about your performance for no reason other than your race.

Different Yardsticks

In the opening example, Shanice found herself smack-dab up against that ever-changing yardstick that comes with some supervisors. You know, the yardstick that can create an attitude problem where there wasn't one before. The yardstick that says white men are expected to project confidence and certainty about all things, to stand tall as pillars of strength and integrity, to be relied upon at all times and reliable in all circumstances. On the other hand, blacks, particularly black women, are supposed to be humble, self-effacing, ever knowledgeable about the opportunities they've been given (as opposed to earned), and grateful about the possibility that they'll be allowed to progress. While this is a sexist thing that all women can face, it's also a black thing.

A survivor probably would not have been in Shanice's position in the first place. For a survivor, the best way to handle this situation would be to significantly reduce her own self-evaluation. Even if a survivor thought she should have gotten a top-of-the-line evaluation, she would have given herself ratings of three with an occasional sprinkling of four thrown in to allow the supervisor the luxury of either boosting the evaluation or reinforcing that the survivor probably wasn't as good as she wanted to be. The survivor's motivation would be not to rock the boat or put herself in any position that would cause her supervisor to increase the spotlight on her.

Now, the striver in Shanice's situation probably would have seethed inwardly but redone the self-evaluation, bumping down her ratings according to how much she wanted to please the boss. The striver would have figured that Patrick would bump down the evaluation anyway, so this might be a way to work her way back into her boss's favor. Since a striver is motivated by getting ahead, the best strategy for her would have been to sit down with Patrick before changing the evaluation to get a real sense of Patrick's concern. Was it Shanice's overall high rating or some specific area that Patrick was concerned about? In doing so, Shanice would send the message to Patrick that she wanted to be fair to herself while addressing his concerns.

Depending on the temperament of the thriver, she would have either gone ballistic on Patrick then and there or done it on paper. Either way, the average thriver wouldn't change one word of that self-evaluation if she believed it when she wrote it. A thriver's motivation is usually to operate from internal integrity, even if the form of that integrity clashes with her superior's. Some thrivers would attempt to take the militant approach of making sure that they did not looked punked in the eyes of a white man. Other thrivers would just believe they were indeed that good.

What Shanice, who normally operates as a striver, did was to flip into full-throttle thriver mode. She told Patrick that she wrote what she believed and that if he wanted to write an evaluation that reflected his differing opinion then he should do so. Shanice also made clear that she would provide a written response to his evaluation if she had any significant disagreements with it. The end result? Let's just say Shanice received an evaluation from Patrick that pretty closely resembled what she wrote about herself.

Shanice completely recognized that she took the chance that Patrick, as a form of revenge for her standing up for herself, could have written a very bad evaluation. What Shanice counted on was that he was going to stay in the neighborhood of fair, and in doing so he would find himself having to write her a great evaluation. At the same time, Shanice affirmed that if he did not do so she was willing to go to the mat, because it was ridiculous to expect her to lower her opinion about herself because Patrick had an issue with her confidence. For Shanice, while it would have been wonderful to have Patrick apologize, the reality is she knew it was gutsy to say as much as she did to him. In the end, she knew the bigger victory was having her evaluation accurately reflect her work accomplishments.

When I read this part of the book to a black male friend of mine, he raised this question: Where do black men and white women fit in the workplace power hierarchy? Good question. Well, the answer is that they are lower than white men, hence the reason why white women, black men, and black women (in that order, according to federal government statistics) make less money. Later that night I brought up the question at a party where there was a good mix of people to survey. My survey reinforced what I always thought—white men are at the top of the power hierarchy. Black men have the double-edged sword of being men—which means they're expected to be bold and confident—but they're also black, so there better be a close correlation between what they say they can do and what they can actually do. White women have their own baggage—they've got the privilege of the right color but the disadvantage of the wrong genitalia. As for black women, well, as a friend of mine (a white lesbian) once said, you're not considered dressed for success in the workplace unless you're wearing a white penis.

While my friend was right that looking and acting like the person who supervises you can help a lot, I don't believe you're screwed if you don't. If you go in thinking like that in every job, you will develop a premature attitude problem that will affect your self-esteem and your work.

Blacks Are Judged by How the Whites in the Room Feel

Although it isn't directly a workplace issue, the controversy involving Professor Henry "Skip" Gates's arrest in his home by a Cambridge police officer in 2009 underscores how, no matter how many whites may think otherwise, blacks feel they are perceived differently at all times in word, deed, and attitude.

Since there was no video camera recording the actual events as they happened, we'll never know exactly why Sergeant Crowley was inside Professor Gates's house after the report of the break-in. We'll never know who actually escalated events to the point where Crowley arrested Gates for disturbing the peace (charges that were dropped the next day). But we do know that blacks and whites had very different views of the facts.

A CNN poll taken shortly after the incident asked the question: "Do you think a white homeowner would have been arrested if he had acted the same way in the same circumstances, or don't you think so?" While 66 percent of whites polled believed a white homeowner would have been arrested, only 25 percent of the blacks polled believed that. In the same poll, when asked if "you have ever been treated unfairly by the police," only 6 percent of whites said that they had versus 56 percent of blacks.

President Obama sparked controversy because he initially said that Officer Crowley "acted stupidly." Many whites were outraged that the president would rush to judgment on this matter, while many blacks snickered to themselves because they knew that finally there was a man in the White House who knew the real deal instead of what white Americans wanted to pretend it was so they could look and feel better.

In other words, blacks and whites tend to perceive these things differently because blacks and white generally have different experiences in the world. And that blacks and whites can have such different perceptions of how people behave in public, widely discussed issues, such as the Gates-Crowley matter, can explain why behaviors and attitudes at work are seen through such different lenses.

Before I wrote this book, I knew this chapter on attitude would be the one that got to the heart of what makes the working experience for blacks in the workplace different than it is for others. Many people who have read *Working While Black* have analogized that the issue of "difference" is the same for women, for gays, for anyone who shows up in the workplace who is not a fully abled, white, heterosexual male from a Judeo-Christian background. But again, it's the issue of attitude—everything else is an offshoot of this issue—that really distinguishes the experience of blacks.

As a writer and a speaker, I never cease to be amazed at the impact of words and the power of phrasing. After talking about *Working While Black* to hundreds of people who shared even more with me than what I knew before, I came to a conclusion that can be succinctly reduced to: black people are judged by how they make the white people in the room feel.

When I said this for the first time at a speech in front of approximately sixty suited, well-coiffed black professionals (with a small sprinkling of nonblacks) in Dallas, Texas, the roar of agreement from the group resembled that from a room full of Jayhawks watching the University of Kansas score a key basket in a championship game.

I've seen hundreds of evaluations of employees, and it is ridiculous how often a black person's personal demeanor, good or bad, is mentioned—even when it technically has nothing to do with his or her job. It is certainly in far bigger proportion than the number of times personality, demeanor, or attitude is ever mentioned in the employment files of white employees. Even the compliment of "articulate," disproportionately used to describe a well-spoken black person, is indirectly a way of saying with barely disguised surprise, "He speaks as if he has some education and thus is not a typical black person whom we should find suspect." I'm not saying every white person who describes every black person has that unspoken subtext, but many times that is exactly what it is. Particularly when used in a situation where the black person should be articulate, since his or her background and qualifications aren't any different from any similarly situated white person.

So how do black employees deal with that hidden, even subconscious job expectation that's tacked on to all the job functions they're actually paid for? A starter is just being aware of this and not letting it sweat you. It happens. The good thing is that not every white person will feel this one. If the election of Barack Obama has taught us anything, it's that many people, especially younger whites, are familiar enough with blacks to not evaluate them based on how comfortable the whites feel.

If there is some objective you're trying to achieve in the workplace, other than merely collecting your paycheck, you might start being more vigilant, noticing how people generally react to you. Do people get quiet when you talk, but not in a "I'm hanging on every word you say because you are so smart and powerful" way, or do you notice people tensing up when you speak? Check your volume or have a person whom you trust—preferably a white person—give you feedback on how others respond to you to make sure that you are not contributing to a negative perception. Because no matter how unfair the perception may be, it's still one you are living with at work.

Measuring Up

The one place white men and black men can easily bond is over sports. It's all out there—who can throw the ball higher, harder, or with better precision is the purest, simplest kind of objective reality. White men can stand being bested at things that involve sheer physical prowess. It's no coincidence to me that white males can deal with black sports figures in a way that they can't seem to deal with black men in any other arena of their lives. My point is that, for example, a white male does not have to feel threatened that Michael Jordan or Kobe Bryant can shoot a basket with more grace than it's ever been done. That can be written off as genetic, physical prowess. To the average sports-drenched male, athletes are practically fictional characters; but let the casual (or real) evaluation process take place, where white males sit around discussing how others in the workplace do their jobs, and the objectivity shifts to radical subjectivity with the white men as the standard.

A great example is the use of the word *token*. It's like the phrase *affirmative action*. They are usually terms used by whites to dismissively explain some positive job action that has happened to a minority. "Jimmy was made vice president of marketing because they needed a token black in the vice presidential ranks." "Marcia got picked to second chair that trial because they just needed a black to look good to the jury." "Beau was put in charge of the night assembly-line shift because of affirmative action, you know."

It's amazing how little analysis whites do, especially white males, when a white person gets a promotion or any kind of job benefit. Competence is assumed, fairness is a given—if you point out that sharing the same skin tone as the decision maker plays a part, you will quickly hear the catchphrases "chip on your shoulder" or "playing the race card." On the other hand, when the script is flipped, not even a whiff of unfairness can be allowed if a white employee is on the losing end. As an employment defense attorney, I've encountered a running joke at the firms I've worked at: the plaintiff in an age discrimination case is probably a white male. You see, in a federal age-discrimination case, a person over the age of forty can file a claim if he believes he's suffered adverse employment action in favor of someone under the age of forty. One of my favorite things to say was, "I wish I had until the age of forty before I suffered from discrimination. I'd still have a few more good years left."

Because I am a black woman who has done plaintiff work (and has personally dealt with bouts of discrimination in my own life and the lives of my loved ones), I'm usually one of the few employment defense attorneys who can detect the kernel of truth in what a plaintiff claims, even in some of the more outrageous lawsuits.

What whites often don't realize is that hearing demeaning, dismissive comments about "tokens" and "affirmative action" can take its toll over the years. Some people have those wonderful personalities that can deflect that kind of negativity. Most of us have to build defenses to deal with it. Unfortunately, part of those defenses can come across as if you are carrying a boulder (rather than a chip) on your shoulder.

All Kinds of Ignorance

A lot of the perceived attitude problem isn't about the black employee at all; it's about the person who is doing the perceiving. Truth is, whites are not always very good at reading the moods or facial expressions of black people. It never ceases to amaze me that the frame of reference many white Americans have for blacks comes from watching *Good Times* or *The Jeffersons* on television. Aside from having to know white people inside out, blacks folks aren't much better at knowing much actual, factual information about other ethnic groups. Many of us only know about Hispanics from watching *Chico and the*

Man, and many of us don't know anything about Native Americans other than claiming that we've got some Native American blood, which is why we have "good hair."

Blacks, on the other hand, can't afford to enter the workforce with the same level of ignorance about white America that whites can have for every other minority group.

In the year I wrote the original edition of this book, I had to explain to my white coworkers, at different times, who Lauryn Hill, Luther Vandross, and P. Diddy were. Can you imagine me going to work and saying that I had never heard of Gwyneth Paltrow, Garth Brooks, or Richard Simmons? They would look at me with disbelief, amazed at how I managed to make it to a professional career with such cultural ignorance. They would say Gwyneth and Garth and Richard were "mainstream," and how could I pick up a newspaper or magazine or watch television without hearing of them? Didn't I see *Shakespeare in Love*, Garth's NBC special, or Richard's *Sweatin' to the Oldies* tape on the Home Shopping Network? Yet I've encountered white coworkers my age who have never heard of *Jet* magazine, don't know that Luther's *Never Too Much* is a classic, and don't remember P. Diddy from when he was sampling as Puff Daddy.

I once saw a grown woman on *Who Wants to Be a Millionaire* blank on the question, "Who is the Queen of Soul?" I remember asking how any game show contestant over the age of thirty could not know that Aretha Franklin is the Queen of Soul. I'll admit, a lot of white folks probably scratched their heads at that one, too.

Granted, my grandmother might not have known many of these black references either, but at the time she hadn't been a member of the workforce for about twenty years and got most of her cultural references from watching old Western movies on

television. With a note of exasperation in her voice, my grandmother Cliffie had to ask me in the summer of 2000 who exactly
this "Harry Potter" was and why everyone on television kept
mentioning him when they spoke.

We are all ignorant of others. Period. No matter how many
seminars, workshops, or mandatory training sessions we go to,
there's only so much we know or can be expected to know about
someone who has a different frame of reference than we do. A
few months ago, a male coworker and I were leaving a restaurant. I was responding to something he said while walking and
then realized that he wasn't beside me anymore. I looked back,
and he was helping a mother get her stroller through the door.
We both saw the woman at the same time, but I didn't even stop
to think about helping her. Never crossed my mind. I have no kids
and have never struggled with a stroller in my life. My friend,
however, has three kids—one a toddler—so he instinctively identified with the woman, her problem, and the solution. Race and
culture are a lot like that. As a society we're trained to be more
culturally sensitive, but here's the bottom line: you can't teach
instinctive cultural awareness.

The level of ignorance allowed by whites in the workplace is one
of the reasons why a lot of black employees have an attitude
problem. Not every black person believes that every white person is ignorant, but blacks can be resentful that this ignorance
can be so open and blatant. When the majority of the people you
work with don't know the names of the top pop-culture figures
with your skin color (unless the person has gone completely

mainstream), it takes its toll on you. For most blacks, this is an example of how whites don't have any interest in knowing anything about blacks unless it directly benefits them.

During a diversity committee meeting for a newspaper I worked at, the topic was what things we needed to emphasize in order to recruit more black journalists. After hearing a whole lot of talk about the outlets for entertainment and the number of blacks who already worked at the paper, I had to ask the editors, "What do you use to attract nonminority candidates to apply?" One editor replied, "Oh, well, the great school system, the arts community, the fabulous housing market, and the beautiful weather." One of the blacks in the group promptly piped up, "Well, black people have kids, like the arts and good weather, and have to have some place to live, so maybe we should mention that."

Black in Charge

In general, many whites (white supervisors in particular) have never had to deal with black people before entering the workplace. What took me by surprise in law school was the number of people who have never had to deal with a black person in authority—not a relative, teacher, family friend, minister, or police officer. They never had one person of color hold power firmly over their heads. I could tell by the complete and utter contempt a handful of my classmates exhibited whenever one of the two black professors dared to call on them in class. While I mention this one example, I've had many whites express that they didn't deal with a "live" black person for the first time until they were adults. While blacks have broken many barriers, statistically speaking, my point isn't a reach. For example, if blacks comprise only 11 percent of the workforce, and of these only 18 percent hold managerial or white-collar jobs, it's fair to say that many whites might go a long time before encountering a black occupying a position of authority. I remember one white coworker sharing with me his surprise at encountering so many black professionals when taking a business trip to Detroit. Coincidentally, another white coworker explained to me that she didn't like the movie *Boomerang* because she felt it was unrealistic that everyone who worked at the company in the movie was black. She said she liked movies better and found them more realistic when whites were more prominently featured. Such a division would more accurately reflect the environment she grew up in and was familiar with.

I came to understand that with power and authority comes fear, and with certain kinds of fear comes respect. Notice I said "certain kinds." If I fear you're going to steal my purse or rape my sister, then I'm not going to respect you. But if I fear that you have the power to flunk me, fire me, punish me, or otherwise alter my life, then subconsciously I'm going to have a healthy respect for your ability to change my reality.

If you've been taught that a certain group of people are not deserving of power and you never see a member of that group wielding that kind of power, then it is harder for you to respect members of that group—not just as bosses, but as peers and even as subordinates. The effect of this on a black person is a heavy, pervasive feeling of never being good enough no matter what you do—a feeling that, for many black employees, blossoms into resentment and anger.

A favorite quote of mine from author James Baldwin is "Not everything that is faced can be changed, but nothing can be changed until it is faced." How do survivors deal with this attitude problem? They usually don't deal with it much at all. Attitude is not an issue for survivors. They are the black employees who go to work and keep their eyes on the prize, so to speak. Survivors appreciate having a job in the first place and remember that every job has problems.

Strivers only start getting an attitude when they get so beaten down by the prevailing system that they have no alternative. The two professions I've been in—journalism and law—both have strong black national professional organizations, with local chapters in larger cities. I've seen many black strivers—too busy to come to meetings when succeeding because they thought the groups were a little too militant—suddenly become poster children for civil rights the second they personally get screwed over.

As I wrote earlier, thrivers are usually slow to develop the "attitude problem" because they usually come in the door with personalities that let their employers know they see the world differently. As thrivers get older, that works more to their benefit, because employees get less reactionary when an older black thriver speaks his mind. However, when a thriver believes problems have gone completely over the top, he might be just the one who waltzes over to the EEOC (Equal Employment Opportunity Commission) office to file a complaint. Mentally, it is a short leap from not being a company guy or girl to being a non–company guy or girl who sues.

Think White, Think Right?

Another place where strivers (not to mention survivors and thrivers) can find themselves dealing with the slap of cultural clash is on the issue of judgment. Bad judgment is a first cousin to the attitude problem. The exercise of good judgment is an implicit part of any job you do. It is also the collective umbrella of subjectivity that probably most drives black folks crazy in the workplace. Often judgment is nothing more than comparing how I would have done something to how you would have done something; and if you're the boss, your judgment trumps mine.

Jessica was a full-blown striver who worked as an accountant. Jessica had a great education and was ambitious, smart, and pretty, with a very likable, laid-back personality. One day she got a nasty e-mail message from a client while she was out to lunch. The client, an East Coast white man, didn't like the way Jessica had communicated an issue about his account. Jessica didn't appreciate the tart tone of the client's e-mail, so she forwarded it to her boss, Frank (who is white). She suggested that he talk to the client and smooth his ruffled feathers, since she was offended by the man's comments and thought it more appropriate that Frank deal with him. Several weeks later, when Jessica was having issues with Frank on an unrelated matter, he brought up her "bad judgment" in how she had handled the client's complaints. Frank was of the opinion that she should have called the client immediately and apologized.

Jessica, on the other hand, was blown away by the fact that her judgment was criticized, figuring that if she had called the client that day with any inkling of a tone in her voice, then she would have been called on the carpet. More important, as a black woman, Jessica felt that in no way,

shape, or form had her firm empowered her to take it upon
herself to make a bold move like that with a client who was
already angry. Frank's insistence that, in her place, he would
have done that sounded to Jessica like an Olympic athlete
with a gold medal in swimming telling a person on crutches
that he should have jumped into a pool to save a drowning
child.

Power. Empowerment. Lack of power. Powerlessness. Those are
the issues that dictate the attitude you have as a black person
when you go to work in the morning, if you let them overwhelm
you.

By the time Jessica was done talking to Frank, damn right
she had an attitude. She had the attitude that she was tired of
being on the bottom of the totem pole, below everyone else at
this particular job (including the brothers), and of being given
the black woman's workload of low-sizzle assignments and mar-
ginal involvement. The combination of being both black and a
woman intensifies the issue—remember, black women make less
on the average than everyone else, including black men. When a
problem came up, was she supposed to put on her superhero suit
and operate like Batman or Superman, when she was neither
white nor in possession of a cape?

So, what were Jessica's options?

First of all, Jessica's initial instinct was a good one. Handling
this fool of a client required thought and finesse. That's why she
had to figure out her objective. Sometimes what happens with us
black folks is that we confuse validating our instincts with meet-

ing our objective. In other words, we need to worry less about being fronted and more about covering our butts. The automatic degree that every black person should have at work—to cover both 85 percent issues and 15 percent issues—is a CYA (Cover Your Ass). The theme of this book, in a nutshell, is that as a black employee you stand out, whether you're a survivor, a striver, or a thriver; therefore, covering your butt is even more important if you want to be a driver, because a black backside is easier to pick out of a lineup.

That's where the motivations of the survivor versus the striver versus the thriver come into play. A survivor would probably be mortified that this was a problem at all. A survivor's motivation would be to make sure that the boss didn't find out about this unless absolutely necessary, so the survivor probably would pick up the phone immediately, hunt the client down, and play nice-nice until she was certain that everything was smoothed over. Then the survivor would mention the incident to her boss in a very minimized or incidental way on the off chance the client mentioned it in passing.

The striver, in his or her motivation to get ahead, would take the approach of hunting down the boss immediately to explain the situation; but a true striver would have a plan of action in full effect first. The striver would not hunt down the boss just to whine or vent but to propose a specific approach to the problem. The striver brother or sister would also make clear to the boss that it was the boss's decision to make.

A thriver would handle it depending on just how pissed off she was and whether this was a last-straw or out-of-the-blue situation. If it was a last-straw situation, where the thriver brother or sister had been tired of dealing with the client's attitude for a while anyway, then the thriver would probably fire off a response by e-mail, or call directly if he or she could reach the client, and call it a day. He or she would not knock him- or herself out telling the boss, figuring that the client's diatribe was a personal problem and not something that the boss needed to be bothered with anyway.

Each of these types would have handled it based on his or her inherent motivations: the survivor to not be blamed for any negative fallout; the striver to not have this incident affect his or her goals to get ahead; and the thriver to not let him or herself be treated badly for any reason.

"Respect" Is More than an Aretha Tune

Another reason why blacks have to deal with the "attitude" problem is that culturally, we generally place a higher premium on being respected than whites do. I consider it an offshoot of living in a society where the *n*-word was an agreed-upon way of addressing black folks and black men were supposed to be OK with the fact that they could openly be called "boy."

Lenora had a job as a communications specialist in her department. Richard was the only other person in the department who held the same title. When it was time to decide who was up for a review, the supervisor told Richard that everyone with his title was exempt from a review that year. The only problem with that decision was that the supervisor had scheduled Lenora for a review the upcoming week. When Lenora questioned the decision, her boss hemmed

and hawed on why Richard was exempt from a review and
she wasn't. In the end, he ended up giving both of them a
review, which just fueled Lenora's suspicions that she was
unfairly receiving harsher treatment. Lenora's boss later
wondered why she had an attitude problem.

Lenora was a thriver. That's why she called her boss on his blatant discrepancy. Because Lenora had strong self-esteem, she
didn't assume that her boss was trying to say that she needed to
be criticized about her work and Richard didn't.

Unfortunately, the so-called attitude problem that we black
folks get saddled with is a defense mechanism to keep from inter-
nalizing our perceptions of how we are being treated. Attitudes
sometimes exist so we can express our discontent with our
employers as opposed to commit out-and-out insurrection. One
way that blacks express their attitude problem is by operating on
the infamous "colored people" (CP) time. While our chronic late-
ness is in great part a cultural issue, in the workplace it can be a
passive-aggressive way to express our attitudes toward our
employers.

In the end, the power structure of the workplace is why the
attitude issue rears its ugly head in the first place. Sometimes it
results from the frustrations of dealing with institutionalized
racism, and sometimes it is just a perception on the part of whites
regarding any negative display of emotion on a black person's
part. Aside from when it manifests itself in an objective fashion,
a lot of blacks just get tired of being graded at work on how we
make the white folks in the room feel. Ultimately, that's what the

attitude problem is about. It's about feeling as if we are judged disproportionately by the reactions we inspire in others. In other words, you feel threatened, so I appear to be angry. You feel nervous, so I appear to be sullen. You feel intimidated, so I appear to be icy.

Despite all our good reasons for indulging in bad attitudes in the workplace, we can never let those attitudes crush us. Sometimes it will show. Life at home is bad—you've got money problems, health problems, marriage problems, or kid problems—and the last thing you want to hear is your boss heaping another problem on your plate as you see him throw loving accolades to your white coworkers. But showing your anger, frustration, fear, or hurt is not an option ninety-nine times out of one hundred. Do not let your attitude ruin your experience. At the very least, don't let it show; because once you do, you become your attitude, and your attitude starts to define your experience.

No matter how hard it is, no matter how many reasons you have not to, never go to work with a demeanor that expresses anything short of "I'm glad to be here, and you should be damn glad to have me." With that attitude, you can roll through whatever comes up.

10

LAW AND ORDER, OR WHAT TO DO
IF YOU DECIDE TO SUE

■

Malik was a fast-food worker at the local food court in a small town with a thriving casino industry. One day while he was working with Patty, his overweight white coworker, Patty criticized something Malik was doing. He responded by saying, "Stay out of my business, Nanook, you killer whale." Patty shot back, "At least I don't look like a black monkey hanging out at the zoo." Phyllis, another white coworker, overheard this and laughed. For the next few months, Patty and Phyllis teased Malik and referred to him as "Monkey Boy."

As I said at the end of the last chapter, attitude rules. No matter what kind of attitude others try to assign to you, you should go to work with your head held high, proud to be a working black. But for some people there comes a day when they've got to take their attitude to another level. There are times when, whether survivor, striver, or thriver, that 15 percent difference becomes your entire work experience and you can't take it anymore.

To Sue or Not to Sue

In the example cited, you've got to wonder if Malik had the basis for a lawsuit. It all depends. Many questions have to be asked. How many employees does Malik's employer have? Under state and federal law, employers cannot be sued for discrimination unless they employ more than a certain number of employees. Was this the first time Malik was teased about his race? Did he laugh or join in when he was teased, or did he tell the teasers he found the comments offensive? Does his workplace have a policy regarding complaints? Did Malik complain according to the policy? If Malik hasn't complained, does his employer even know about the racial teasing? What does Malik want? Does he want the teasing to stop, or does he simply want an apology? Does he want Patty and Phyllis fired? Is Malik just after money, and, if so, how much does he want? How much could he get?

As Whitney Sings, "How Will I Know?"

Deciding whether you should bring a lawsuit against your employer is one of the single most important decisions you'll ever make. You can't take it lightly, because as my employment law professor said, if you bring a lawsuit against your employer, some-times even when you win, you lose. His point was that while you may have the law and the facts on your side (or at least on your side enough to convince a jury that you're in the right), you've put a nice little red-and-white target squarely on your back for your next employer. Not to mention the protracted stress you inevitably put yourself and your family under to get that mythi-cal, beloved jury verdict in your hands.

Here's the funny part. Most people sue because, at some level, they want the world to know that their bosses are racist, bigoted jerks. They also want to be vindicated for every indig-nity they believe they suffered and show everyone that they are heroic for helping prevent this from happening to anyone ever again. At the very least, the less altruistic blacks who sue figure that everyone deserves to know how much cash they were able to milk from the bloodsuckers who screwed them over.

But most lawsuits are settled out of court. This means that no one is going to know anything about how wrong your employer was, because 99 percent of the time you and your employer will sign a confidentiality agreement stating that you can't tell anyone about the settlement *and* that the settlement isn't an admission of guilt on the part of the employer. More impor-tant, many confidentiality agreements have what is called a "liq-uidated damages" clause, which means that you can be taken to court and essentially fined a set amount of money for each time it can be proved that you spoke about the agreement. These amounts can be anywhere from one thousand dollars per instance on up, depending on the size of the settlement and how big a badass your employer or former employer wants to be. That's one sure way to convince people to keep their mouths shut, and com-panies know it.

That's why it is really important to sit down and examine what your intent is in making a complaint and the best way to get that complaint heard. If you want it to be official, put it in writing to your immediate supervisor and copy the people above him or her. If your company has an internal grievance procedure, follow that to the letter with no personalized variations. If you work in a more informal environment, ask your boss to lunch and try that approach.

How you start is how you finish. If you're going to be a driving force in taking the lawsuit avenue, date and document everything. If possible, always think in terms of problem resolution rather than revenge or getting even. You always look better when you take the high road, and if you ever do find yourself in front of a judge and jury, the side whose case looks better is usually the side with the better chance of winning.

Why Some People Seek Legal Advice

When things are going badly at work, you feel as if someone has pushed you into a corner and is building piles and piles of wet sand that you can't climb over, can't see under, and can't breathe through. You know that if you don't get out before the last pile of sand has been built in front of you, you'll die of suffocation if you don't perish from hopelessness first.

At some point, it all merges together—fear, hopelessness, anger, depression, and apathy. You get to the point where you can't think about your job situation, you can only feel the heaviness of it. Thinking rationally about your job, your pay, the place you work, and the people you work with becomes harder than lifting weights at the gym; and when even one other black coworker shares your pain or feels that strain of despair, you have confirmation in your heart and head that you're being screwed. The only question is what to do about it.

That's where suing comes in.

When it feels that bad, that unfair, that just plain ol' wrong, you go right to the place that says, "Sue the bastards—sue the bastards for everything they have and make them feel this same pain." But taking that step requires you to know that the ground ahead could be quicksand rather than sweet, firm earth.

Marissa worked at her company as a mail handler. She started off in the mailroom at the age of eighteen and was still at the same job in the mailroom approximately one college degree and eleven years later. Because she was ready to start making more money, despite the fact that her job in the mailroom was super easy, she decided to apply for other jobs in the company. She felt, with her degree and years of service, that the company owed a black woman the chance to climb the ladder.

The company found it easier to give bright new college graduates a job in middle management than to give a higher-level job to someone who was, at best, a mediocre mail handler. After getting passed over for one too many jobs, Marissa filed an EEOC complaint for race and sex discrimination. Then she hired an attorney and filed a lawsuit. The case eventually went to trial. Marissa won in a jury trial and was awarded $23,000 in actual damages and $3.5 million in punitive damages. Her company appealed and won, with the appeal going all the way up the circuit. The court reduced her award of damages to $43,000, half of which she had to give to her attorneys in fees and expenses.

From the day Marissa filed her EEOC complaint to the day she walked out of her attorney's office with less than $20,000 was approximately four and a half years. And, oh yeah, she still worked for the company as a mail handler.

When it comes to pursuing legal remedies in your job, it's necessary for you to be the most careful driver of all. Complaints, especially ones that may lead to litigation, are not tactics to be taken lightly. You don't get to pick and choose how people will react, and regardless of how many laws there are forbidding retaliation, paycheck signers will not appreciate a lawsuit while you still work there. Supervisors will act nervous, and coworkers may suddenly act weird around you for fear they'll be called as witnesses or dragged into the lawsuit somehow. So you have to ask yourself what you're driving yourself to achieve. Vindication? Peace of mind? Money? To be heard?

The destination decides the route. For example, if the destination is simply to be heard and to alert your employer to a problem, then you can sit down with your supervisor or with someone in human resources. Note that while the law protects you against negative employment action arising from your complaint (legal retaliation), it doesn't protect you from someone feeling annoyed, resentful, or defensive; do not sit down and take that route if you're the kind of person who lacks the ability to deal with contention.

If you feel that your problem is one of those 85 percent issues—workers' compensation or the Family and Medical Leave Act, for example—that is when you need to go talk to someone in human resources to get your questions answered. When it comes to one of those color-free issues, you're always better off getting your information right from the horse's mouth rather than assuming that there will be racial implications.

If you feel that what has been done to you is based on race and you find it particularly egregious, go for broke and file an EEOC complaint. Again, you've got to ask yourself what that will net you after the time and energy you will have to give to that process. When you do feel driven to that point, the hardest thing to understand is that no one is ever going to apologize to you for his or her discrimination or racism. Doesn't happen. Therefore, if you're trying to get yourself a winning jury verdict, know that it never comes with a "You were right, I was wrong, and I'm sorry" attached.

There's Law but Not Always Order

Real-life litigation is not like the movies or television. Fake drama gives you no indication of just how time-consuming, grueling, and emotionally taxing suing your employer can be. It's amazing how many employment laws exist. There's the Family and Medical Leave Act (FMLA). There's the Americans with Disabilities Act (ADA). There's workers' compensation. There's state law. There's local law. There are a whole bunch of laws out there. When it comes to racial discrimination, the federal law primarily used is Title VII, which came about as part of the Civil Rights Act of 1964. Title VII prohibits job discrimination against employees on the basis of race, color, national origin, religion, and gender at any stage of the employment process. But there are a range of other laws and remedies that can also affect you as a black person— those applying to gender, age, pregnancy, retaliation, and more.

Back to Marissa. She got the satisfaction of taking her case to trial. She got the emotional payoff of having a jury find in her favor, with millions of dollars added in punitive damages to make it really hit home. But what Marissa learned along the way is that when David meets Goliath, it's more like David meets Hotshot, Superior, and Paid LLP, Goliath's litigation team, who bills by the hour and has an arsenal of pistols, cannons, and smoke bombs at its disposal to counteract David's lonely, overworked slingshot.

Sometimes the slingshot can beat the army of weapons. Ask Texaco, Coca-Cola, Adams' Mark, Denny's, and other big companies that have suffered embarrassing and huge losses when employment discrimination claims were brought against them. But a single employee, hiring a solo attorney or an attorney for a small firm (because the big firms almost always represent the employers), needs to have a lot of stamina to fight the good fight.

Peter worked in a big corporation in the Midwest for several years. One day, out of the clear blue sky, Peter was fired. He believed the only reason was because he was black. Even though he was able to find another good job in the same industry, he decided to file an EEOC complaint for the purpose of punishing his former employer. As a pride-filled black man, he felt he had no other choice. Peter looked for an attorney after he got the right-to-sue letter required by law, but none thought he had a good-enough case. (A right-to-sue letter is a legal document that the EEOC is required to provide before a potential plaintiff is allowed to file a lawsuit.) Peter stubbornly refused to believe that and filed the lawsuit himself as a pro se plaintiff. (In legal jargon, *pro se* means that he was representing himself, and every expense had to come out of his own pocket instead of being fronted by an attorney.) Peter was so serious and determined to not give up this lawsuit that even when his former employer offered to settle with him, he said no. He lost his new job because of the time it took to research his own case and respond to every motion from the other side. Peter also lost his condo, both of his cars, and his credit rating because he had to drain his savings and his 401(k) for depositions and other expenses. The last time I talked to Peter a few years ago, he was enrolled in out-of-state law school and still fighting Goliath Inc.

There is no one-size-fits-all method for determining whether to pursue a claim for discrimination. Every person's set of facts is different and laced with just enough nuance to separate it from similar cases.

Peter was a striver who decided to become a full-bodied thriver. Something about what his boss did to him and the reasons given struck him to the core of his being, and he wasn't willing to let it go, no matter how much he had to lose in order to win. Even when the company was willing to settle with him for a decent amount, Peter found it better to risk getting nothing than to get something and have to keep his mouth shut about it. It was a big leap from former company man and striver who had his eye on moving up the corporate ladder to become the chief antagonist in open warfare. A black survivor wouldn't have risked a damn thing to prove a point—let alone a sweet condo and two nice cars—and the average striver would have walked away with the settlement (and the signed confidentiality agreement) ready to make his or her mark somewhere else.

Ultimately, the final decision of how much he was willing to lose was all on Peter. For him, being a driver meant giving up everything he owned so he wouldn't feel as if he had rolled over for mere money. Another black person might have taken the initial settlement offer made by the company, feeling that he might as well take the money because it couldn't change what had already happened. Which is another point that people don't realize. When an employee brings a discrimination suit after he or she has been fired from the job, reinstatement is rarely a court-ordered option.

Legal Discrimination in a Nutshell

I should start off by saying that discrimination in and of itself is not wrong or unlawful. *Discrimination* just means "to distinguish." When you buy a red sweater instead of a purple one, you're using your power of discrimination to make a choice. When you decide to apply for job A instead of job B because job A pays more than what you are making and job B doesn't, you are discriminating between two possibilities. When an employer who is a Jayhawks fan hires me because I'm a University of Kansas graduate instead of hiring a candidate who is a Kansas State Wildcat, hey, I have to applaud the employer's good taste and discrimination. The law doesn't say that employers can't discriminate; it just maintains that an employer cannot *unlawfully* discriminate. Usually the difference rests on the basis of why the person is discriminating (or choosing) between one person or one course of action and another.

The basics start with the law. Almost every state has antidiscrimination laws that prohibit adverse employment actions on the basis of race or other specific areas of protection. Being in a protected class means that you are able to claim legal discrimination based on your membership in that class. The groups that federal laws generally protect are distinguished by race, creed, color, sex, disability, pregnancy, veteran status, and age. I was stunned to discover that not every state prohibits discrimination on the basis of race. I worked on a case once that required me to put in a clause about Alabama state law prohibiting race discrimination. After looking in all the obvious places to find what I thought was a basic fact, I made a call to the Alabama counsel and found that there was no state law. There was a state law prohibiting discrimination on the basis of age, but not race. Hmmmmm.

If you receive an adverse employment action because of your membership in a "protected class," according to Congress, that is illegal. For example, if your boss passes you up for a promotion because you are black, you have received an adverse employment action (being passed over for a promotion) based on your membership in a class (race) the law protects. Now, if you want to bring a federal lawsuit for employment discrimination stating that your boss didn't give you a job because you mentioned in your interview that you're a Yankees fan and your boss likes the Mets, well, you're out of luck, because the law doesn't make sports fans a protected class.

Basically, the employment relationship is governed by the at-will concept. That means that, unless you work under a contract or in a union, you work at the will of your employer. In plain English, you can quit any time you want and your employer can kick you to the curb any time she wants, as long as she isn't firing you for one of the narrowly stated reasons recognized by the law. Although most employment is at will, if you're an executive or a professional in an industry that typically uses employment contracts, you may not be an at-will employee after all. In this case, you need to remember that your contract will govern the bounds of your employment relationship. The key thing to note is that just because something is in writing doesn't mean you're working under a contract. For example, a prospective employer writing a letter offering you a job does not automatically mean you are under a contract. In fact, it usually doesn't mean that at all, and an employer with a good lawyer will make sure the offer explicitly states that the letter is not a contract and that you're an at-will employee who can be terminated without cause.

Once you get the job, however, if your boss is making your life a living hell, that doesn't mean the court will offer you protection. If we're talking about race rather than other forms of legally protected discrimination, then you only have a case if your boss is making your life a living hell because of your race. That is one of the reasons why there is no such thing as reverse discrimination when discrimination refers to whites. While the federal law prohibiting discrimination may have come about because of black Americans, you know a 1960-something Congress was going to make sure that the umbrella included everyone, including white folks. (Not to mention that little "equal protection" thing in constitutional law.) So if a black supervisor keeps passing over the white men in a department because they are white and male, one or all of those men who have been passed over for a job can bring a race and gender discrimination lawsuit. The law doesn't recognize the concept of *reverse* discrimination; it only recognizes discrimination.

Employment discrimination is a complex area of law that applies to a number of different scenarios. In general, Title VII is the primary federal law that governs employment discrimination, and most state laws governing racial discrimination use Title VII as the guideline. Title VII covers private employers; federal, state, and local governments; and educational institutions that employ fifteen or more individuals. Basically, any employee or job applicant who believes that he or she has been discriminated against in regard to hiring, firing, compensation, assignment, transfer, promotion, layoff, job advertisement, recruitment, benefits, or any other terms or conditions of employment has a prima facie case. *Prima facie* is just legal talk that means you have the right to put the needle on the record and start the song.

Other areas of discrimination where a black employee could bring a federal discrimination claim on the basis of race include harassment (also known as "hostile work environment") and retaliation against an employee for filing a charge of discrimination, participating in an investigation, or opposing discriminatory practices. One of the reasons why you should consult an attorney before deciding to take any action against your employer is that the words *discrimination*, *harassment*, and *retaliation* have common everyday meanings separate and apart from their legal meanings.

When I was a solo practitioner as a plaintiff's attorney, I would frequently get calls from black employees saying that their bosses were harassing them and they wanted to know if they could file lawsuits. Often, what they would call "harassment" would be things such as their bosses telling them that they needed to be at work on time, criticizing how they did their jobs, or asking them questions that they thought were none of their business. People didn't want to hear that conduct can be harassing, but the law only protects you if the harassment is based on your membership in a protected class.

Your boss can make fun of the fact that you think mixing plaids and stripes in the same outfit is good fashion sense when you work as a computer programmer. You can feel like she is harassing you because she doesn't say hello to you in the morning as enthusiastically as she does to your white coworkers or because she doesn't like that you use smiley faces when you send e-mails. But the harassment has to be racial harassment for you to be able to take legal action. The fact that you're black and your boss is white does not count. The law doesn't allow recovery for that connection; otherwise every black person would be receiving reparations one lawsuit at a time.

Franklin had been written up for spending too much time on the Internet. He worked in an office job that involved a lot of computer work, and he would frequently jump online to look at the news and sports scores, make travel plans, and otherwise cruise the information highway when he had a few spare minutes—and sometimes when he didn't. Franklin's computer screen faced a part of the work area where his boss could easily see color pictures on his screen. Too bad his job didn't involve color pictures. Franklin felt that he was unfairly harassed because his boss wrote him up for what other people also did. Franklin's boss may very well have been picking on him, but as I explained when he called my office, your boss has the right to make you the example if you're doing something wrong, and most employers find goofing off on the Internet during work hours a problem. This was the only incident Franklin could point to as harassment. Franklin also admitted that the written reprimand probably was not a big deal, considering that he was otherwise an excellent employee and couldn't deny the accuracy of the reprimand. Franklin was just mad that nobody else got in trouble for doing the same thing.

What the law says is that your work environment must be free of racial harassment, and that applies to your coworkers as well as your supervisors if the law feels that your employer could have stopped unlawful harassment and didn't. Examples of this include racial slurs, racial jokes, or any conduct or speech that is "severe and pervasive" and based on your race. (As with just about every aspect of legal discrimination I discuss in this book, while I'm limiting the examples to race because of the focus of the book, the examples also apply to the other protected classes mentioned earlier, as well as conditions covered by your particular state's laws. These may include discrimination or harassment based on sexual orientation, political affiliations, citizenship status, marital status, or personal appearance.)

In the chapter opening, Malik may very well have had a lawsuit. I observed this incident while taking my grandmother out of town, and it was one of those rare instances I got to see a potential discrimination lawsuit unfold before my own eyes. Usually I see the disputed facts on paper long after everything has happened. As a black woman, I was appalled to see these white girls calling this brother "monkey" to his face and laughing. I could see the simmering anger in his demeanor as he quietly made sandwiches, and I could feel his pain of knowing that, while he wanted to slap these white girls silly, in this little town his black behind would not only be out of a job but would be put into the local jail as well.

While my black woman's emotions were processing all this, my dispassionate lawyer's brain wondered about many of the questions I posed at the beginning of the chapter. Unfortunately, declaring a hostile work environment isn't a simple matter. As offensive and upsetting as the behavior of those girls was, if this was the only time something like this ever happened, Malik wouldn't have much of a case if he decided to sue. Worse, what would he really get even if he went to all that trouble? Would it be worth it to burn his bridges in a small town against an influential employer for no more than probably a few thousand dollars? Only Malik would know.

Let's say Malik didn't want to go as far as filing a lawsuit, but he wanted to demand that the behavior stop. Would writing a letter to his supervisor or human resources be a good idea? It depends. It's one of those judgment calls where you have to consider what that will get you where you work. A young friend of mine, a black woman, was being sexually harassed by her boss. On advice from some of her family members, she wrote a letter to her boss outlining the behavior and demanding that it stop. The next day her boss fired her. Yes, that was totally and completely illegal—not just the sexually harassing behavior, but also the firing that would be considered illegal retaliation. But my friend was far too concerned with finding another job to go that route. It wasn't that she was wrong to write a letter, but demand letters—which outline a behavior and demand that it stop—in the hands of someone other than an attorney can be very dangerous.

The advantages to suing are obvious—the chance for closure, justice, punishment, redemption, purging, and, of course, the almighty dollar bill. The news is filled with stories of huge verdicts and companies brought to their knees, but you don't see the negatives in those stories.

In the year 2000, plaintiffs filed more than 259,000 civil complaints in the United States district courts. A *civil complaint* is one where a private individual or group sues another private party, as opposed to a criminal matter where the government brings a matter against an individual. According to the U.S. Department of Justice, about 41,000 of those complaints involved a civil-rights-related issue, such as discrimination in employment, housing, welfare benefits, or voting rights. Of all these civil rights complaints, only 1,652 of them went to trial, with 80 percent of those heard by a jury. The average amount of time elapsed from filing the claim to deposition to trial was fourteen months, which of course does not include any appeal that may have taken place. The U.S. Department of Justice statistics show that plaintiffs (the people bringing the lawsuit in the first place) won only 34 percent of the verdicts in 2000. Of the 545 plaintiffs who won their trials, 76 percent of them were awarded monetary damages, with half of these awards being $155,500 or less.

What these statistics show is that for employees who feel discriminated against and who take their claims all the way through a federal trial (where discrimination lawsuits under Title VII are typically tried), only about one in three is able to convince a judge or jury he or she was discriminated against. Of those who won in court, the average amount of money was not enough to live on for any meaningful period of time, especially when you consider that your attorney will take one third to one half of what you recover. Settlements are much harder statistics to track because they are usually signed under a confidentiality agreement. But my educated guess, based on the settlement amounts I've seen, is that the average settlement is considerably lower than the average amount a plaintiff wins in a trial verdict.

Statistics and chances of meaningful recovery aside, that does not mean that people who file discrimination suits don't make a powerful collective statement to Corporate America. In 2009, the EEOC reported the second-highest number of employment discrimination complaints filed, resulting in a record-high $294 million in payments or penalties through administrative enforcement and mediation. More than one third—36 percent—of those 93,277 claims were based on race discrimination.

As someone who worked mostly on the defense end of lawsuits (which means representing the employers who are sued by their employees), I think a person looking for money and vindication from her employers has only slightly better odds of winning than if she buys five dozen Powerball tickets.

Steps in a Lawsuit

Here's a bare-bones overview of what happens when someone decides to file a lawsuit. Every lawsuit is different depending on the claims filed, the facts, the lawyer you hire, and more. But all lawsuits, regardless of claims, go a similar route. First, you shop around for an attorney. If your case looks good and you're willing to take the time to put in the legwork, you find one to take your case. Either before you find an attorney or shortly after doing so, you file a complaint with the EEOC to preserve your right to bring a lawsuit under Title VII. It's possible to file a discrimination suit without doing so, but it makes a tough burden of proof even tougher if you have to assert a discrimination claim without asserting a Title VII claim. Once you find an attorney to take your case, he spends a lot of time going over the facts with you so that he can file a complaint to start the lawsuit in federal court, which is where most discrimination lawsuits are heard because Title VII is federal law. After your employer files an "answer" to your complaint, then the real paper war (called "discovery") begins. That means that you have to turn over all your documents relating to your claim to the other side and the other side has to do the same for you. Neither side gets to pick and choose what they show—it all comes out in the wash—or else the law prohibits you from using that information if your case goes to trial. It's only in a *Perry Mason* episode where a party gets to come forward with a surprise document the week of trial.

Every evaluation, every memorandum, every e-mail, every company policy, every magazine article you accidentally leave in your desk drawer, every diary entry relating to work is up for grabs. The expense of copying and producing all these documents comes out of your pocket if you settle, if you win, or if your attorney requires it from your contingency agreement (the contract you enter into with your attorney that says his pay is contingent on you acquiring a settlement or verdict). In addition to preparing all that paperwork, you have to answer questions under court orders called *interrogatories* and show up in some lawyer's office to answer questions from your employer's or former employer's lawyers in what is called a *deposition*. In addition to you answering questions all day long under oath, every person you list as a potential witness can also be deposed by the other side's lawyer whether you like it or not or whether he or she likes it or not.

Since depositions lawyers can ask questions in discovery about anything relevant or likely to lead to admissible and relevant information, you will undoubtedly be asked questions about things that you think are none of anyone's business. (A discovery deposition is what happens when the attorney on the other side of the case questions you under oath without a judge present for the purpose of discovering information potentially relevant to the case.) You may not think it is relevant to your lawsuit that you witnessed your scout leader molesting your best friend when you were eight years old, but if you went to therapy over it, the lawyers will question you to prove the point that your emotional distress was caused by your early childhood trauma and not by your boss promoting every white person in the department over you.

In discovery you'll also find out what your coworkers are willing to say under oath (especially if they still work for the company) versus what they're willing to say to you in the break room when the bosses aren't around. In depositions you'll get to hear what your boss will publicly say about you to justify whatever adverse employment decision he made that has him being deposed in the first place. In other words, you'll learn just how he plans to run you into the ground before a jury.

After discovery closes comes the part that most plaintiffs' attorneys don't really bother explaining well to their clients. It's the part where the employer's attorneys write a long, detailed document (that they bill thousands of dollars for) called a "motion for summary judgment" that essentially asks the judge to rule on all the claims without wasting time or money by taking the claims to trial before a jury. If the judge denies the motion for summary judgment, you get to take your case to trial. If the judge only issues a partial summary judgment, that means you only go to trial on whatever part of the case the judge leaves in because there are "disputed facts." For example, if you bring claims of discrimination, hostile work environment, and retaliation, the judge can rule that there is no basis for trial on the discrimination and harassment claims but can leave it up to a jury to decide the claim of retaliation. This means that evidence on everything other than the retaliation charge has to stay out of trial.

The worst phone call a plaintiff's attorney has to make to her client is to break the news that the judge granted the defendant's complete motion for summary judgment. That's an especially hard phone call to make if there was a settlement offer on the table that the plaintiff didn't accept. What the judge's order means is that unless you appeal (an expensive and time-consuming endeavor that your original attorney may not agree to take on), you've lost before the trial begins. It's the equivalent of the NBA commissioner saying before the start of the NBA finals, "Sorry, but we don't even need to have a championship tournament because Team X is so vastly superior to Team Y that it would be a waste of time and money. Even on the off chance Team Y wins, we would still give the championship trophy to Team X." Because summary judgment happens only after depositions and written discovery have taken place, a plaintiff who loses on summary judgment feels a lot like Team X, suited up for a chance to win the big game and not even being allowed to play.

If, as a plaintiff, you survive summary judgment, then you get the opportunity to go to trial. You get the joy of sitting through the grueling weeks of preparing for and enduring one of the most stressful times of your life, while a jury not of your peers (because you will almost always have a mostly white jury in a federal trial) holds the final answer to whether you win, and if so, how much.

My years of representing employers showed me how much more the deck is stacked against the plaintiff from day one if the employer is a big company. Big companies may not like big legal bills, but they will pay them month after month to keep from paying an undeserving plaintiff one dime. With rare exceptions, an employer who is being sued by an employee or former employee never thinks the person deserves anything. When they do decide to settle, it's almost always defense counsel who has to walk them down that road, because employers practically never believe they discriminate and don't want to do anything that concedes that they do—which a settlement does in their minds.

A lot of people think it is unfair that lawyers get to walk away with so much of your money. But hey, let's be clear: if not for your lawyer, you wouldn't have the sixteen thousand dollars in the first place. After all, if talking to your employers by yourself was working, then you wouldn't have gotten demoted, fired, spit on, or whatever it was that drove you to a lawyer's office in the first place, now, would you?

Reverse Discrimination on the Rise

One of the biggest recent changes affecting blacks in the workplace, at least indirectly, is a Supreme Court ruling that supports cases of "reverse discrimination." Now, as I have written, the term "reverse discrimination" is inaccurate, because adversely affecting one's employment on the basis of race, regardless of the race of either person, can be discrimination.

Of course, this ruling complicated the concept. The Court sided with a group of mostly white firefighters from the city of New Haven, Connecticut. In its five-to-four ruling, the majority ruled that the city improperly threw out the results of promotional exams that officials felt left too few minorities qualified. The Court ruled that the city made an impermissible legal finding on the basis of race under Title VII that created disparate impact.

Some lawyers view this ruling as really saying that disparate impact of a test on racial minorities is not, in itself, enough to "reasonably" conclude that the test illegally discriminates against minorities. In order to throw out the test, the employer will have to point to some factors other than the fear of getting sued. This ruling was viewed as an upholding of the "rights" of people in reverse discrimination cases. But in my view, the Court is enforcing the overall policy that it is illegal to have adverse employment decisions turn on issues of race.

With the election of a black president and the appointment of the first Latina to the Supreme Court, I think the Supreme Court's ruling signals a sea change in how the country has come to think about race and racial equality. As whites dwindle in numbers compared to nonwhites—with nonwhites expected to be the numerical majority by midcentury—issues involving racial discrimination are increasingly being raised more by whites.

Now, this could be a good thing—if increased awareness of their own issues of discrimination led to whites' greater sensitivity to the discrimination issues of others. In some cases, I think that will happen. With other groups of whites, however, not only will there not be greater sensitivity, but there will also be greater resentment toward any remaining efforts to equalize the years of systemic discrimination directed against people of color.

Specifically, blacks should be more aware of the importance of watching their language when discussing issues of race in the workplace. It's no longer a matter of whites being the ones who have to be careful about what they say about racial minorities— racial minorities need to be careful too.

For example, even when you know you are talking to someone who feels exactly the same way you do, even if it's another white person, be aware of your surroundings. Lower your voices; avoid the conversations in public places or on your employer's clock. Keep the deep, insightful conversations about race relations to personal encounters, preferably far away from ears that will take even the smallest point out of context.

Also, if you are a black person with authority, make sure that all your personnel decisions are fairly and completely documented. Don't make the mistake of assuming that racial minorities are the only people you have to worry about bringing a racial discrimination lawsuit in the future.

Bottom line for black folks—there are now more whites in the workplace who have more ammunition in their arsenals to try to dismantle attempts to improve the diversity of the workplace. Be fair and be aware.

Your Personality Type and Whether to Sue

When it comes down to deciding whether to file a lawsuit, your motivation really does matter. If you're a survivor, there is no good reason to file a lawsuit against your employer or former employer. It's just going to direct a giant spotlight right in your direction, and you're not the kind of brother or sister who can handle it. You're just not built that way. You want to come and go to work, and the only disruption you want in your work world is if you decide to change jobs. Even that is something a survivor typically wants to do with as little fanfare as possible.

If you're a striver, you better do a fabulous cost-benefit analysis of exactly what it will net you in the short run and what it will net you in the long run; because, as I frequently tell witnesses during preparation for their first depositions, litigation is war, and your guns may not be as big as you think they are. A striver may win his skirmish and end up losing the war. If you're trying to get ahead in your particular workplace or even in the profession or industry you work in, no matter how many laws against retaliation exist, no one's career is going to benefit from filing a lawsuit against his employer.

It won't matter how right you are, and except for rare instances, it won't even matter how egregious your boss's behavior was. You will have broken the code. We in the black community know all about that. As soon as a prominent black man goes down in flames for failing to keep his hands where they are supposed to be (that is, off a woman who is not his wife or off money that is not his own), then our collective community starts pointing fingers at what black woman or white man brought him down. Nobody likes tattletales, no matter how justified the telling may be.

Thrivers are going to lead with heart first when it comes to going the lawsuit route. They don't embarrass or scare easily, so the pitfalls of taking it to the streets don't paralyze them the way they would for their other black coworkers. It's not that a thriver necessarily operates from a higher sense of integrity than a survivor or a striver; in fact, an individual may operate from less. In the handful of times I've seen a black employee file a discrimination claim that I felt was strictly just for the money, it's usually a person I would classify as a thriver, one who has no fear of the downside and retribution that may come her way. A thriver, whether operating from integrity or not, is just not going to care in the end if she only ends up with a settlement of three thousand dollars or a jury verdict of eight thousand if she feels she had her day of glory and theater. She got flair and don't care.

Regardless of whether you are a survivor, striver, or thriver, there are certain bottom-line considerations to be taken into account if you are driven to pursue the lawsuit route. A basic one is to make sure that if you do find yourself feeling discriminated against or racially harassed, you find your company's Equal Opportunity policy and follow it to the letter. In other words, if your company's EEOC policy says that you are to report a complaint to your immediate supervisor or human resources manager, then those are your choices. Deciding that you would rather report the complaint to the nice brother or sister supervisor in another department or to some other employee may be just the out your employer uses to say that he didn't know there was a problem in the first place. (A lawsuit, *Faragher v. City of Boca Raton*, created a defense that allows employers to avoid or reduce liability if they can show that the company had an antidiscrimination policy with an adequate reporting mechanism and the employee failed to use it. Although companies and defense attorneys can use the *Faragher* defense as bludgeon to beat back a claim, I'm a fan of the defense when it is correctly used because it is only fair.)

If you really think that where you worked is whacked, then you should give them a chance to fix it before you run off and file a lawsuit. Yes, you take the chance that you get blown off or treated worse, but you also take the chance that it gets better, not just for yourself but for the other people in a similar situation. This remedy can be a whole lot faster and potentially a lot less painful. Reporting your problems also puts your company on notice that, if it is being discriminatory in some way or allowing a discriminatory environment to breed, it better fix it, because the next time it has to deal with it may be on the responding end of a lawsuit.

I don't believe in idle threats involving the law—more often than not, I think there are better ways to handle situations first. But if you genuinely think that a lawsuit is going to be a recourse you take down the line, the first place you start is with complaining according to your company's policies.

Can You Hear What I Hear?

My observation is that when people have been discriminated against, the thing they really need is to feel heard. They want to feel as if they had a fighting chance to tell their side or make their case or just vent about what they perceive as unjust actions. Employers could cut some complaints or lawsuits off at the knees if they would just have conversations with black employees as soon as they get the information that their employees are having problems regarding race in the workplace. Here, as in other areas of life, so much could be resolved quickly through good communication. When the communication turns out to be not so good, sometimes the song just needs to be sung, even if it's a little bit off-key.

11

BRIDGE OVER TROUBLED WATERS

■

Patrick worked in a restaurant as an assistant chef, working more hours than part-time but not enough hours to be officially full-time. He figured he worked long enough and hard enough to be considered full-time, despite the fact that he didn't get benefits. Patrick believed that restaurants were places where things were worked out informally, unlike some fancy-pants office job where people had a lot of stupid rules and regulations to follow. When Patrick, the only black on the kitchen staff, refused to chop some zucchini because he didn't think it fit in the featured entrée, the head chef tried to send Patrick home for the night. Patrick argued back and got fired on the spot. Worse yet, when he tried to get unemployment benefits, he found out that he was ineligible because he wasn't a full-time employee at the restaurant. Plus, even if he had been a full-time employee, because he

got fired "for cause" he still wouldn't have received that
weekly unemployment check.

Head First or Feet First

Sometimes, the best thing that can happen to you is to get fired.
Believe it or not, what can seem like the single most humiliating,
painful, scary event in your life can be the most liberating. You
don't want to make it a habit, and it's certainly not something you
brag about on your resume, but it sometimes happens. When it
does, you pick yourself up and move on.

I got fired from my first job out of college. I carried my
happy black behind halfway across the country to work for a big
city newspaper and left four months later, hating the city, the city
editor, and the newspaper. I know that the experience was the
first step toward learning that while I loved to write and to meet
and talk to people, I wasn't cut out for the structure of the daily
newspaper business. Because I was so young and it was my first
job out of college, I didn't spend any time considering whether
being a reporter brought me joy or if I was great at it. I just got
another job doing the same thing elsewhere. Sometimes a firing
is a gift that can be a blessing in disguise, but that's only if you
pause long enough to look at what the blessing really is.

As I write this, an acquaintance of mine works for a company that has laid off the equivalent of a small town in the past
year. He is probably one of the only ones who is mad that he has
avoided four different rounds of layoffs. Why doesn't he just quit?
Because his company is offering generous severance packages,

enough to finance his beloved dream business, and he would rather have that than quit and get nothing but a last paycheck. He's a thriver disguised as a survivor, so when his layoff comes— and it surely will—he'll see it for the blessing it is.

There are only two ways to leave a job—you quit or you get fired. Sure, technically, you could be laid off or your company could go under or you could retire; but any way you slice it, if you're an at-will employee you either do the electric slide out on your own, or you start hearing the slow jams come on at the end of the party when you know your host wants you gone.

I've always envied people who have employment contracts. They have defined, clearly identified periods of working rela- tionships—usually a year, when the rubber meets the road (unless one of the parties wants to reenlist, so to speak). Most working Americans will, as at-will employees, have more haphazard rela- tionships with their employers. From day to day, week to week, month to month, year to year, you wonder if the blade hovers over your neck. Or you don't worry and then, seemingly out of the blue, the guillotine slices your head off anyway.

I'm always amazed, however, at the black people I know who operate without a healthy strain of paranoia in the workplace. Recently a friend of mine, in a fit of rage, threw a coffeepot at a coworker. Hot coffee and flying glass went everywhere. A medi- ation was scheduled. In between picking up shards of glass and waiting for the mediation, brother man never wavered in his belief that everything would be fine and they wouldn't fire him. He threw the coffeepot at a white coworker for using the *n*-word in front of him, and his only concern was that his boss would try to force him to shake the white guy's hand. The combination of losing a job at the age of twenty-one and seeing employment lit- igation lawsuits every day left me in awe of my friend's calm. He was right. He didn't get fired, but I still think he needs to look over his shoulder.

This chapter is for figuring out how to survey the lay of the land when you're ready to bounce, you just got canned, or you expect that it is coming around the corner.

Skin Is In, but What Color?

The funny thing about race in America is that most whites think our black skins protect us from getting the pink slip, with the general assumption being that employers don't want to court a lawsuit. (Pardon the pun.) In comparison, many blacks feel that our skin color makes us stand out when the workplace executioner comes looking for bodies.

Assumptions don't matter. Reasons matter even less when your employer decides to put your head on the chopping block. Any way it happens, it feels like a dull knife.

On the other hand, deciding to leave under your own steam is a tough decision too, if you're leaving because something smells rotten in the apple barrel. Most people who leave for new jobs with more money, more prestige, and more everything and absolutely love their work probably aren't reading this far into this book.

In the workplace, as a black person, you have a lot of considerations when it comes to job security. I've mentioned people who are survivors throughout this book as if there is only one kind. Some people are survivors because their natural attitude is one of temperance. They're the people who usually drive the speed limit, pay their bills on time, and do all the right things at the right times for the right reasons. When that type of black survivor gets the boot, it's usually a performance issue, pure and simple. If you're the kind of black survivor who is working in a fundamentally fair place, you won't get fired until your performance becomes problematic enough to register on your bosses' radar screen. (There are times when straight-up racists target survivors anyway, but fortunately for these types, strivers and thrivers make more attractive targets because they are "uppity" blacks.) For someone who typically operates as a survivor, getting the ax for a performance issue can seem like the end of the world, because it symbolizes the ultimate mark of personal failure.

For blacks who typically operate as strivers and always look for the next opportunity to advance, being fired can seem like someone is hauling them right off the ladder of success. Even though thrivers tend to be the most standout kind of black in the workplace, I've always found that strivers are the undercover militants, especially when they get fired. You see, strivers—unlike thrivers—are the ones who bought into the concept that hard work is enough and the blacks who complain about racism are just making excuses. Strivers think that right up until they get the ax or the demotion, and then they practically want to march on Washington.

Back in the day of the forefront of the civil rights movement (and before), black Americans wrestled with the issue of assimilation versus desegregation. In simplistic terms, someone who wants to assimilate wants to morph her differences into the collective mainstream. "I'm not a black architect; I'm an architect who happens to be black." Someone who is a fan of desegregation isn't trying to blend in, she's just trying not to be excluded. "I don't care whether you view me as a black architect or an architect who is black, I just want to make sure my black behind has a fair opportunity to be admitted to architecture school." When a striver realizes that the playing field isn't fair and assimilation isn't taking, it can get ugly. In other words, when a striver has to ask Langston Hughes's age-old question, "What happens to a dream deferred?" she begins to feel betrayed and bitter and wonders if the societal promises of fairness and equality are nothing more than a raisin in the sun.

A black thriver (who usually is about two beats off the company tune anyway) may not be as surprised by a termination when it comes, but he's usually more upset that the white man has the power to put him in the ultimate one-down position. A black thriver, depending on his personality and temperament, will more visibly and directly proclaim just what he feels about his job, his supervisor, and the screwing over he feels he's getting. It's not that thrivers are immune from being surprised by a termination. A thriver can get totally sideswiped too. It's just that his reaction of surprise usually won't be a product of naivete or trust. A thriver has great clarity about the politics of the workplace and his place in that dynamic, both individually and as a black employee.

Red Flags to Cover Your Butt

What are the red flags that warn you that termination may be coming down the pike? Operating as a driver means paying attention to these warning signs. They may seem obvious, but I am always amazed at the people who say they never saw the firing coming and then, after asking them a few questions, you realize they were just straight-up living at the intersection of Denial Road and Oblivious Boulevard.

Red Flag #1: Criticisms from your boss suddenly start showing up in writing, when criticisms were previously verbal or informal.

Actually, any switch in communication style from your boss should alert you that something is up. If your supervisor, for example, is the type who stops by your work station to talk about your work and then she suddenly starts using e-mail as her primary means of communication, look at the circumstances to see if you should be worried. Like most things in life, it's all about context. For example, if your boss changed to an office farther away, acquired new duties, or is going through a divorce, the switch to e-mail may just be circumstantial. But if you see her still communicating freely with Jake, your white cubicle neighbor, chances are there is something up with you.

Basically, if your boss starts communicating with you in writing or you start a new job and find yourself receiving written criticisms left and right, you need to consider the possibility that it may be a warning sign of bigger trouble down the road.

One of the key things an employment defense attorney relies on in building a defense is the personnel file of the person bringing the discrimination lawsuit. Unfortunately, the more your personnel file is filled with write-ups, reprimands, and written warnings, the easier it will be for the employer to show a legitimate nondiscriminatory reason (one of the legal standards) for doing whatever it is you are suing over in the first place.

Therefore, don't take changes in communication and increased negative feedback lightly. They mean something. They may mean that your boss is overworked or is pissed at you because you spilled Grape Nehi on the rug at his house during the company party, or they may mean that you work for someone who likes to exert his "Boss Authority" on paper every chance he gets.

Ask questions about the change in communication style, or ask the person communicating differently some questions. If the answers leave you with a funny feeling, let your fingers get busy typing up Monster.com to start shopping for another job (or at

least another job in the company) once you determine that it's a
you thang rather than a general dissatisfaction that has nothing
to do with you.

Red Flag #2: Your key alliances start to undergo changes or your
supervisor changes.

Another red flag that is a lot less obvious than the good ol'
paper trail is when key alliances start to undergo changes or your
supervision changes. What most people don't like to hear, or
admit to, is that it does not matter if the supervisor you've had
for twelve years loves your work. If the next supervisor doesn't,
that can be enough to create some rough waters for you.

No matter what color you are, the bottom line in the workplace is that you are only as good as the last person who evalu-
ates your performance says you are. I've seen situations where a
really harsh supervisor took over a department and fired a black
employee, who then filed a race discrimination claim. The fired
employee attempted to use as evidence the fact that she had glowing evaluations, or at least average ones, until she got this racist
supervisor. What usually happens is the company defends itself
by saying the new supervisor was a stricter evaluator. In other
words, the defense becomes that your glowing reviews all the
years before weren't so glowing; you just had an easier boss. That
means it's not discrimination when your new boss hates you.

Unfortunately for you, a paper trail as tall as the pyramids
can be built behind your back. Your boss doesn't necessarily have
to tell you about it or show you the blizzard of nasty comments
going on behind closed doors. I know of one brother, a computer
specialist, who found out by chance that his boss was planning
to pull the plug on his job. He came across at least half a dozen
documents outlining not only the how, when, and where, but the

details of why—including allegations that he knew nothing about. His job search instantly jumped up to number one on his "to do" list.

Obviously, this can also work in reverse, too. You get so-so performance reviews for years and then you're lucky enough to get a new boss who just loves your work and gives you great reviews. If you're a driver, you capitalize on that. You use the timing of the better, smarter supervision (because if you look better on paper, the evaluation process had to improve, right?) to figure out what more you want from that job. A supervisor or boss who loves your work and finds your personality a pleasure is a thing of beauty.

When things don't look so good, the point is not to turn into a paranoid wreck who is looking around every corner anticipating a problem or a firing. It's also not about itching for a lawsuit or finding the best way to get back at your boss if you do get fired. In general, it's about heeding the warning signs when you see them and having a general idea of what your rights and responsibilities are.

Some people have learned just enough about retaliation laws to cloak themselves in protection by filing complaints with the companies or the EEOC when they get a whiff of trouble brewing. Sometimes filing a complaint can slow down the clock and buy you some time to either find another job or work out whatever problem has come up. Other times, your goose is already deep fried, so filing a complaint just gives you another claim to tack on to a lawsuit.

Red Flag #3: Your job or duties change.

When your individual job starts undergoing changes that are not company or department-wide, that might mean you are showing up on someone's radar. I think that is particularly true if your area and level of responsibility shift down instead of up. The change could signal that your boss is trying to say that you're not doing your job well or that someone else can do it better. When your work responsibilities shift up, that's when you need to look at your circumstances individually. In most cases, it's a sign that your boss trusts you, and that's a great thing. In some cases, it's a sign that you're being set up to be broken down. Again, there is no blanket way to know if that's the case other than listening, watching, and observing how others are handled. If your job is changed altogether to a lateral (or lesser) position, then you really need to take that as a red flag that something hinky may be going on. It's one of the things that can be an 85 percent issue or a 15 percent issue. In other words, you've got to investigate the underlying reason for why this is happening and what the future implications of it are.

What You Can Expect When You Leave

If you're not fired and you choose to leave, what do you have the right to ask from your employer? Every state is different, but employees are entitled to what they accumulated up to the point they quit. By that, I mean that your boss can't get mad at you if you quit and, as a form of retaliation, not pay you for the work you did last week. Your boss can decide, however, that the day you turn in your resignation is the last day she wants you working, and she has no obligation to allow you to work past that day.

Tanya worked at a fast-food restaurant as a cashier. She told her manager she was quitting to go work for another fast-food place that paid a higher hourly wage. Her manager told Tanya that, despite her two weeks' notice, he didn't want her to come back once her shift was over. When Tanya came back to the restaurant a few days later to collect her last paycheck, her manager had failed to include payment for the last week she worked. Tanya called a lawyer, saying she wanted her pay for that last week plus the two weeks she was willing to work. Her lawyer informed her that under state wage and hour laws she was entitled to the last week of pay because she actually worked to earn it but that the law doesn't require you to be paid for time you didn't work. Since Tanya was an at-will employee, her boss had the right to cut off her continued ability to work for that employer.

Unless you are under a contract that requires it, the whole concept of two weeks' notice is a courtesy, not a legal requirement. That's why, even when I have a good relationship with an employer, I quit before I quit. By that I mean I erase all personal e-mails from the system, get rid of private items from my hard drive, and make sure that any personal documents I've casually thrown in my desk drawer are taken home without drawing attention to the fact. The other day, some friends of mine, black and white employment defense attorneys, were joking about how you could guess when we were about to quit. I said if you saw the picture of my grandmother, mother, and dog gone, I was out. One guy said his diplomas off the wall would be our first clue. The other guy said check to see if the photos of his wife and daughters were missing. Another friend jokingly said her office would be gutted.

Take a tip from the employment lawyers. If we clean house first, that might be a good idea for you, too. Because of the type of law we practice, we're aware that you never know how your boss is going to take a resignation and that the day you give your two weeks' notice could be your last day, period. In fact, if things are shaky at work, it's best to start making the slow, unobtrusive movement of stuff from your workplace to your home. You may get zero advance notice from your boss if she decides to ask you to leave, and sometimes she may barely allow you to get your personal belongings, under her watchful eye, before she escorts you from the building.

I remember how one day, when I was a newspaper reporter, a black female editor was called to the managing editor's office. When she got to his office, she was surprised to find herself fired. What was more surprising to her was that she wasn't even allowed to go back to her desk to clean out her personal items—she was escorted out of the building and a white female editor was sent to retrieve her purse and give it to the fired editor at her car. I wasn't close to the editor and don't know if she saw the firing coming, but if she didn't, she lost all ability to shield her personal items and papers from prying eyes when her box of private things was sent to her. She also lost access to any pertinent information she might have wanted to print out should she have wanted to file a discrimination claim.

Cash Out Benefits or Forfeit Them

In addition to any pay you've earned, you need to look at your company policy to see if you have any unused vacation time or if you get paid sick leave. Remember, none of it is a given. It's all dictated by a combination of state law and company policy. That's pretty much all your company is obligated to give you once you tell them you're hitting the road.

In Missouri, my home state, we have a statute that requires an employer to furnish a "service letter" when you leave employment, regardless of how you leave. Generally, the letter serves as a statement from your employer saying that you worked there, giving your job description and your dates of employment. That could come in handy for an employee who gets fired or quits and needs to verify employment but doesn't want to list anyone from the company as a reference. (Of course, in volunteering a letter like that to a prospective employer you may be sending the company a red flag that you can't get a good reference from your former employer. Depending on your individual circumstances, you may decide to take that chance.)

Unemployment Benefits Don't Benefit All

Unemployment benefits are governed by statutory law. According to the Department of Labor, less than 40 percent of jobless Americans were able to receive unemployment benefits in the year 2000. For one thing, in just about every state, quitting your job does not entitle you to unemployment benefits. Also, if you receive a severance package from your employer (usually just the equivalent of your pay for a set period of time, such as one week for every year you worked or a flat two months), it can affect the size of your unemployment benefits and the length of time you receive them. Severance payments are typically deducted from unemployment benefits. Many states also look at the reason why you were terminated to decide if you are eligible. For example, if you were terminated for a reason that would basically be considered a crime, also known as "felonious conduct," you might not be eligible. (Note: Because this is almost entirely governed by state law, it is nearly impossible to know just from reading this chapter whether you would be eligible for unemployment benefits in your state.)

Is a Severance Package in Your Future?

Let's say you get offered a severance package, or you've been terminated and want to know if you're eligible for a severance package. It should go without saying that if you are fired for doing something that would land you in the penitentiary, then you're probably not going to be in the position to ask your employer for another dime, other than what they already owe you. I know of a case where an employer caught an employee putting some of the employer's product into the employee's car on company time. Unfortunately for the employee, it wasn't the employee's job to load product, and it certainly wasn't in his job description to load it into his own car and drive it home. One pesky, well-placed video surveillance camera caught the employee's beautiful profile, and his job became nothing more than a line on another job application. Did the employer offer the employee a severance package? Indirectly. The employer didn't offer the employee money, but he graciously didn't call the police and have the man arrested. I'd call that a good severance package.

On the other hand, if you're getting terminated for poor performance and you truly believe that it doesn't pass the smell test, ask for severance. For example, if you're the only black person in the department and the boss seems to be overlooking the performance deficiencies of your white coworkers, your employer might be willing to talk severance to keep you from filing a complaint or lawsuit down the line. Of course, the size of the severance will almost never be enough for you to retire on. It might be two weeks' or eight months' pay, depending on how vulnerable the employer feels, and you'll almost always be asked to sign a release that waives all future claims and lawsuits.

Is it worth hiring a lawyer to try to get a better severance? In most cases it is not, unless you are in a situation where you believe the intercession of an attorney would get you several more months' severance than doing it on your own. Truthfully, most of the time I think it wouldn't be worth the expense, since whatever you get is split with the attorney. When I was a plaintiff's attorney, I had a client for whom I was able to negotiate an eight-month severance package because the employer had done such a bad job of firing the man that it started to look like something other than performance might have been the real issue. If the man had not hired me, he might have only gotten two months. But in hiring me, by the time I took out my cut and expenses, he really only received about four months of severance. For him, it was worth it, not just from a financial standpoint but to make it a point of pride with his former employers that he wasn't going to give them a free pass for unfair treatment.

The lesson I learned from that experience is that people don't have very realistic ideas of what it means when they hire lawyers. Hiring a lawyer totally changes the dynamic. Sometimes it makes it a lot worse, because your employer or former employer is so pissed you took it outside that he becomes totally inflexible. But sometimes he becomes so intimidated or irritated that he'll throw a little more money at the situation to either make it go away quickly or keep it from escalating into a much more public, much more expensive showdown. In any case, merits don't have a whole lot to do with the final outcome.

Unless you're leaving your job for more cash or more cachet, it's never easy to leave. If you get fired, it never feels good, regardless of how necessary the break was in the big picture of your life. If you leave because you're unhappy, especially because you feel you didn't get a break because of your race, that feeling can seep into your soul and leave you unsettled for years to come.

As I said at the beginning of the book, how you start is how you finish—and I believe that how you finish can affect your next start. If you can, make choices that leave you with dignity and that allow you to walk out on your own terms. Even if that doesn't happen and you find yourself walking out on your employer's terms, you always have the right and the duty to yourself to walk out with your head held high.

12

FEELING DOWN BUT NOT OUT

■

Next to the CEO and the vice president, Edward is the highest-paid person in his Fortune 500 company. There are only a small handful of black executives in the country that have Edward's kind of juice or make his kind of bank outside of the entertainment and sports industries.

Although Edward sometimes works sixteen-hour days and frequently has to travel for his job, the one thing he always does is take his five-mile-a-day run. Period. Without fail. Whether he's at home or in Hong Kong or Paris or Toronto, he exercises his body, knowing that his mind and spirit are stronger because of it.

How you start is how you finish. It applies to so many things—relationships, jobs, new situations. As I've gotten older, I've realized that the saying is more about the spiritual than the physical start to a new beginning. If I go into a work situation believing I'm doing the exact job I'm perfect for, then chances are when I leave the job or get promoted or transferred, it will be a better ending or transition than if I started off that same job feeling like I was lucky to even get the interview in the first place.

Ultimately, your job isn't just one part of your life; it is a reflection of every choice you've ever made. I make this bold statement because I believe everything is connected to everything else. It's no coincidence that ambitious, hardworking people, regardless of race, make more money than people who desire nothing more than doing the least amount of work for the most amount of money. Sure, there are lazy CEOs who are born into wealth and hardworking janitors who develop calluses from what they do. My point isn't about deserving what you get, it's about getting what choices create, even the choices that seem unrelated to that job.

Edward runs his five miles every day because, ultimately, he is an instinctive striver who aims to be a driver. He knows that to keep his mind sharp and his goals sharper, he has to have an outlet for stress. He also knows that as superficial as it may be, a fit, healthy black man will command more respect from everyone he deals with than one who looks like he can be toppled by one more helping of fast food or one more cigarette.

I began this book by saying that a black person in America needs to start thinking about what makes her or him happy before she or he enters the job market. While you can change your mind midway, there is just no reason to be on a path you hate if you give thought to who you are and what you want from life.

Last year I started doing yoga. At the start of every class, Kathleen, my yoga instructor, starts off saying, "Set your inten-

tion. Say your prayer for whatever you need from class today."
When Kathleen asks that, I have to consciously think about what
I need for that class. Stamina? Energy? Flexibility? Just to get
through class, even though I might feel like a soft bed or a cool
drink would be better? In a nutshell, setting your intention is
what you have to do as a black person who wants to succeed in
the working world. You don't just set your intention once. You
set it every day, every year, and at every stage of your career. As
you grow and change, your intentions grow and change. Whether
you are a survivor, a striver, or a thriver, intention is the one thing
always within your power, regardless of the dynamics that you
do not control. Intention is what turns a survivor, striver, or
thriver into a driver, and intention is one part of your work life
you do have the power to control and nurture.

Throughout this book I've addressed the 15 percent difference that defines being a black person in the workplace; however,
I never lose sight of the fact that we are all 100 percent human.
No matter how many ways you define yourself, keeping mental,
physical, emotional, and spiritual balance should be your top priority for maintaining a healthy work life. At the end of the day,
no one can tell you exactly how to deal with your boss, company,
or employer. So much of what it means to be black in America,
especially a working black, is to accept and not feel crushed by
the fact that the dynamics are so much larger than you are. Maintaining a healthy balance in your life will help carry you through
the hard times and help you succeed during the good ones.

Yesterday I heard a white secretary complaining; she was
upset about a computer freezing up. The same day I got a call
from a friend who is a black attorney; she wanted me to help cal-
culate the likelihood of her being fired by the end of the year.
Stress may be stress, but from where I sit, it seems that whites at

work usually get stressed over tangible irritations. While all employees get stressed out over concrete annoyances such as freezing computers, black employees often pile on top of that the added stress that the subtle but powerful nuances being a minority in the workplace generates.

Society will indeed be equal when black people have the same peace of mind that whites do so we can just let life happen without the added stress of hidden agendas constantly tugging at the edges of our consciousness. We still live in a society where being black is a consideration that impacts every aspect of our existence.

Walter, a black accountant, was in a low-grade panic because he had been having trouble with Jennifer, his white supervisor. Walter sent Jennifer an e-mail requesting permission for the go-ahead on a time-sensitive project, and she hadn't responded, despite the fact that the two of them had passed each other in the hall several times and chatted in the company cafeteria. Jennifer had even responded promptly to Walter's e-mails regarding other current projects. When Walter finally mustered the nerve to ask Jennifer directly about the new project, Jennifer said yes without hesitation, stating that she had just forgotten to get back to Walter. Walter read Jennifer's lack of response as confirmation of his lack of job security.

E-mail makes many people expect to hear back from others more quickly and feel slighted by others who don't respond promptly. But blacks suffer from obsessively thinking we're out of sync with what's going on with our white supervisors.

In some ways, this is the most important chapter of this book, because this one's all about you and the things you can control to improve your life, whether you're a survivor, a striver, or a thriver. You can file every complaint, bring every lawsuit, and fight every fight, but you can't control the outcome. As a driver, however, what you can control is your ability to live your life without compromise in an environment you can alter but not fix.

In other words, you can learn to control your response to what you can't control, which is similar to the serenity prayer used in twelve-step programs where you ask your higher power to grant you the serenity to accept the things that can't be changed, the courage to change the things that can be changed, and the wisdom to know the difference. That should probably be the workplace mantra for blacks, too.

I've read more than once that when a pilot flies, he spends most of his time correcting the flight plan while navigating between takeoff and landing points. This is because between wind, weather, and dozens of other subtle yet significant factors that can't be predicted, a pilot has to spend much of the flight correcting any deviation that takes the airplane off track.

As a black person in America who works, keeping on top of a healthy, balanced lifestyle is critical for moving forward and keeping that 15 percent difference to a minimum. Trying to maintain that healthy balance becomes a necessary way to constantly set your intention and keep on course.

Internalizing Is a Form of Depression

Depression and job stress can lead to quiet, unconscious ways of taking yourself out of this life early.

I think one of the reasons that black Americans are disproportionately more religious than the rest of America is because the hope of a better afterlife is what many of us have been led to hold onto. Most of us have to believe in this concept of a better world beyond. We had to believe that as slaves, we had to believe that during Jim Crow, and we especially have to believe it now, when everything is supposed to be equal but we see every day that it's not. How can we survive today, in this world, in this life—if we look at the routine, unblinking, unthinking, unrepentant discrimination that we deal with daily in every area of our lives—if we don't cling desperately to the idea of hope?

I've attended too many funerals of my people where that was exactly the theme of the eulogies—that the pain, hopelessness, and the life of struggle would reap us our rewards on the other side. Rap and hip-hop aren't anything more than modern-day Negro spirituals sung by our youth.

A white coworker of mine came rolling into my office a few years ago, full of chitchat about the fact that the D.C. sniper was a black man. "Didn't see that one coming," was the sentiment he expressed and the one expressed all over the country. After all, it's not a "black crime" to shoot randomly or murder serially. Nope, we do garden-variety black-on-black crimes, with a few smash and grabs thrown in to break up the monotony. I pointed out to my coworker that white America might want to be a little scared that this might start a trend. After all, most of the employees and former employees who shoot up workplaces because they feel they've been treated badly are, statistically speaking, both white and male. Just think what would happen if blacks who felt treated badly in the workplace took up guns instead of EEOC complaints. He left my office muttering, "It would be bad all the way around."

Fortunately for America, but unfortunately for black Americans, we take our stress, anger, and hopelessness and turn it inward. According to a recent study, blacks have higher death rates than whites for eight of the ten leading causes of death—heart disease, cancer, stroke, unintentional injuries, flu and pneumonia, diabetes, HIV/AIDS, and cirrhosis of the liver. David R. Williams, a sociologist at the University of Michigan Institute for Social Research (the world's largest academic survey and research organization), says that the racial gap between the health of whites and blacks is no different now than it was in 1950; he in part links that gap to "the historic legacy of racism."

Not to be flip, but that makes sense to me. If I can't hit my boss for being a racist jerk (or at the very least an insensitive one), my blood pressure is going to consistently go up, which increases my risk for a heart attack or stroke. If I constantly see my white coworkers treated with grace and dignity through every screwup while I know my mistakes put me one step closer to the firing line, chances are that I will tend to smoke or drink more, eat more, or act more recklessly when I'm away from work, which increases my risk of cancer, heart disease, accidents, and so forth. You get the point.

Blacks have higher mortality rates than whites until the age of eighty-five, according to the National Center for Health Statistics. The disparities between blacks and whites in morbidity include blacks being three times more likely than whites to have diabetes and having a 40 percent higher rate of heart disease. The infant mortality rate for blacks is twice that of whites, regardless of education, marital status, or income. It doesn't take a PhD to know that living a more stressful life without healthy outlets leads to more stress.

That's why, as a black community, we tend to get only part of the equation better than the rest—we work on the spiritual aspect but often let the physical, mental, and emotional ways of dealing go unchecked. Being black is a full-time job. Blacks get hit with it all—a higher incidence of bad health, lower access to good health care, and more stresses to start the vicious cycle all over again. In fact, studies show that blacks of all income levels tend to get less attentive medical care than whites.

So how does that relate to work? Easy: the one thing that contributes most to an unhealthy lifestyle is stress. You know how it goes. If you're stressed, you look for an outlet to relieve it such as smoking, overeating, taking drugs, gambling, overspending, or getting abusive. A study that came out of Finland in 2002 said stress can double your risk of dying of heart disease. The study showed that people who reported persistent stress due to work, low job security, or few career opportunities had the same level of risk for fatal heart attacks as people who smoke and don't exercise. Apparently, high job stress was associated with being overweight and having high cholesterol. That might explain why, compared to the overall population, blacks have more weight problems and higher cholesterol. I don't know about the folks in Finland, but I do know that if you're black in America, you got stress all the way around.

So you have greater stress in your life. Now, what can you do to help yourself do battle at work when necessary and to have the emotional, spiritual, and physical stamina to carry on all day, every day?

Working It Out While Talking It Over

Marissa is a time bomb waiting to go off. She's a thirty-something black employee who works for the government and has had half a dozen screaming matches with fellow employees who are all black. Her supervisor, a white man, keeps ordering mediations and in-house counseling sessions. Marissa is on edge, and everyone who works with her is on edge when they see her temper about to flare. Everyone assumes it will take Marissa going off on a white person for the boss to really do anything about it. She clearly needs to seek out a mental health care professional. It might be some physical or psychological problem that causes her to act out, or it may be that Marissa is just a bitch. Either way, she needs to have someone help her get a grip. Without taking a serious dip in the anger management pool, Marissa is in no position to stave off dealing with any work-related difficulties that come her way.

There are certain cultural realities that plague our community and put us at an even greater risk for stress. One is that we tend not to seek out help when we need it or even to think we need it in the first place. "I ain't crazy." "I'm not talking to some white person about my problems." "It's nobody's business what I'm thinking." "It's not that bad." "Therapy and that kind of foolishness is for white folks." "I'll just pray on it." "I can handle it."

Prayer is great. So are supportive friends and family. Our own internal strength is the best of all, but sometimes we need to seek out another person to talk to—a voice from outside our daily life to give perspective.

If you don't do it because it's good for you or because you might need it, think of it from a legal perspective. Juries award for damages. The bigger the damages, the bigger the monetary award. Damages have to be proved. One of the ways you can prove damages is by showing you were so mentally and emotionally traumatized you had to seek therapy. Therefore, if you decide to seek out a counselor or therapy, don't look at it as the boss or white folks driving you to therapy. Look at it as the natural aftermath of a stressful injury. If you got hit by a car or came down with a painful physical disease, you wouldn't look at it as moral failing because you had to see a doctor. That's the way to look at excessive stress.

I've always felt that, with the higher level of stress and abuse black Americans go through, therapy should be free for anyone who seeks it out as a tax the rest of society has to pay. But I know that one very true concern about going to seek therapy is that when you're stressed from every direction, the last thing you want to do is bare your soul to a white person. Not only do you want someone who automatically understands what you're talking about, you just don't want to be in the position of being judged by yet another person not of your own background. You're not willing to give someone that kind of power.

There are black mental health care providers. You have to look harder for them, but they exist. (See the resources section for a helpful Web site.)

Spiritual Journey to Keep You on Your Path

As I said, many blacks count themselves as regular churchgoers. What if you're not? Am I recommending going to church? Nope, not at all. I personally think that everyone needs to find her own basis for spirituality and do whatever it is that nurtures her soul. If Jesus Christ is your path, then find ways to incorporate more of that path into your daily work life. In other words, don't just go to church on Sunday. Become more active in your church or do more volunteer work. Perform your own set of spiritual rituals that makes you feel like your time on this earth matters and that collecting that paycheck isn't the only use you have. One friend of mine is a church usher and finds that her regular church attendance and other activities help her cope when she goes to work, because she feels she is working as an instrument of Christ.

If you're not a Christian, don't let Christians make you think that it's the only path to salvation if you're black. Explore other options, whether that is a New Thought community, Buddhism, Islam, or Yoruba. Don't let the majority (which includes the majority of black people) stop you. If you need to chant or say a mantra before you go to work in the morning, do it. It's nobody else's business who that chant is to or what it includes.

Religion is one of those no-no topics to get into with blacks if you're not exactly on the same page. If you don't believe in God or a higher power, then look to something that provides spiritual sustenance. If it's not the Bible or Iyanla Vanzant, then do volunteer work. Seeing a whole bunch of people who are less fortunate than you are is a good way to put work stresses in perspective, as well as build some spiritual muscles you might have forgotten you had.

Your Body Tells the Whole Story

Another major area of our lives we have to put more of a priority on is the physical. As black Americans, we can't afford to go to work at anything less than optimal health because, as that Finnish study I referred to earlier concludes, people with more job stresses already have double the risk of heart disease.

At least the federal government is getting hip to the fact that it's ridiculous there is no better overall health care for blacks than there was fifty years ago. The U.S. Department of Health and Human Services (HHS) drew up a federal mandate in 2000 that said by 2010, health care disparities should be eliminated. Starting in the year 2003, the National Institute of Health no longer reviewed grant proposals for studies that don't say how they will include minorities in clinical trials.

In terms of being proactive, we black Americans have to do our part to make sure our employers can't hit a moving target—and if we're getting exercise, we're moving. It's harder to take down or run over a healthy man or woman than it is an unhealthy, sickly one. Getting fit and staying fit allows you to be in top shape to manage your workplace experience. That's why we have to walk, run, bike, hike, or dance to music on the radio. We've got to shake our moneymakers if we want to make more money and live long enough to enjoy it.

Smoking cigarettes doesn't help us either. In 1998, the HHS said that approximately 29 percent of blacks smoke. That's almost one third of us engaging in a destructive activity that just nets us easier access to strokes, heart attacks, and all the other things that just don't seem to hit whites nearly as early, often, or hard as they hit us.

Obesity is another one of those preventable risk factors that affects us more than any other group because we use food as the great equalizer. We eat more and have worse eating habits. We like our chicken greasy, our potatoes buttery, and our vegetables cheesy. And we better have dessert, starting with sweet potato pie and ending with whatever is our mama's specialty. One of the tolls obesity takes on our community is the epidemic rate of adult diabetes. According to a report in December 2001 from the National Diabetes Education Program at the National Institutes of Health, of the 15.7 million men and women currently diagnosed with diabetes (a number that increases by roughly 800,000 new cases each year), more than half are women, and half of those are black. Those high numbers are attributed to the rise of obesity, lack of exercise, and the fact that people are living longer overall.

The Black Women's Health Imperative reported that out of every one hundred black women, sixty-seven are overweight and thirty-eight of those overweight are considered obese, which means they are 20 percent or more above their ideal body weight. How does this relate to being black in the workplace? Unfortunately, higher stress without healthy ways to cope leads to unhealthy habits and excessive worrying. Eating is a form of stress relief, so it's easy to see how sitting on a couch worrying instead of working through stress physically relates to the fact that the death rates for blacks with diabetes are 2.5 times higher than for their white counterparts.

Another physical manifestation of stress is high blood pressure; studies show that black men twenty and older have nearly twice the likelihood of having high blood pressure as white men of the same age. High blood pressure is a major heart attack risk factor. According to studies cited in the book *The Black Man's*

Guide to Good Health, racial discrimination can be a cause of stress that can lead to high blood pressure.

Strong Mental Health Makes Us Stronger at Work

In an ideal world, the good life of fatty food, tasty liquor, and minimal exertion—with a few cigarettes and recreational drugs thrown in for good measure—would have no impact on health, stress, or vitality. But that's not the case. If you're battling workplace stress, here are a few tips based on what the statistics say particularly affect black folks:

1. Get regular checkups. You may be more stressed than you realize, and a doctor might be able to help nail down ways your stress manifests itself that you aren't even aware of.

2. Take an honest look at the ways you self-medicate and why you do it. Don't fool yourself if you know you eat, drink, smoke, or engage in any harmful activity to excess as a way of distracting yourself from work-based insecurity or discrimination.

3. Stay active. Running your mouth and jumping to conclusions are forms of daily exercise, but they are not the kinds that help counteract deep-seated stress. Walk, run, bike, dance, take a class, or pick up a sport. Pound that ball, burn up that pavement, or punish that boxing bag. Let the unchecked adrenaline course through your body.

4. Get more sleep. When you're overly stressed, you often have trouble going to sleep, or you don't sleep soundly when you do go to sleep. Sleep deprivation doesn't make the day go any better

at work. When someone is working on your last nerve and it's not a well-rested nerve, you might find yourself having inappropriate responses that will just make everything worse. According to sleep researchers, most people need sixty to ninety minutes more sleep than they get.

5. Engage in less "groupthink" and more "what do I think." In general, we black people are very much into the collective. I recently had a conversation with a black newcomer to Kansas City, Missouri, who was asking me why he never saw black people at this location or that location. He mistakenly thought there were a lot fewer blacks in the city because of this. I pointed out all the places that are "in" for blacks to go to and that unfortunately the places he liked to go weren't "in" for blacks at that time. Part of our stress comes from our assumption that if a large number of blacks say something, it must be so, from music to restaurants to religion to public opinion on an issue. We all have a responsibility to rely on fact rather than sheer opinion for the sake of our peace of mind.

6. Set goals. Don't just set goals in your head; write them on paper and make them specific. Make some easily attainable and small— for example, update your resume by the end of the month—and then set some that allow you to reach beyond your immediate grasp. For example, you could open your own jazz bar by your forty-fifth birthday. Writing down your hopes and dreams and the steps you can take toward those hopes and dreams helps you to feel less at the mercy of your employer. It's part of the spiritual component of knowing that you are part of a bigger plan.

The smartest, most successful black striver can find himself smack in the middle of stress overload. The Bible says that to whom much is given, much is required. Those higher requirements can bring on greater stress. In other words, some blacks have stress overload from dealing with discrimination and problems at work; other blacks have it going on so much and so well that the stress from carrying the heavy load of societal success gets to them.

Studies have shown that the short-term effects of stress on performance include the following:

- Interference with judgment
- Difficulty making good decisions
- Reduction in work enjoyment
- Seeing difficult situations as threats rather than as challenges
- Promotion of negative thinking
- Damage to self-confidence
- Narrow attention
- Disrupted focus and concentration
- Difficulty coping with distractions

All the ways that stress can manifest itself are ways that can impair your work performance, and impaired work performance makes you a more likely target for your boss. All in all, it's a vicious cycle for anyone to be caught in, and it's particularly deadly for a black person to be caught in. That's why it is so critical to get a handle on stress when it rears its ugly head.

"The Runaway Slave"

When I told a friend of mine, a black woman in her fifties, about the topic of this book, she suggested that I have a chapter about the "runaway slave" for blacks who think about working for themselves or starting their own businesses.

She's got a great point. Leaving the white work world is an option. Unfortunately, it's not one that many of us have a lot of experience thinking about. When I decided to open my own law firm, I had no role models for how to start a business. I had worked for others since the age of fourteen; I was the daughter of a lifelong federal government employee and the grandchild of people who had always worked for other people. What I learned from the experience of working for myself is more about mentality and courage than anything else. There are books and Web sites where you can gather advice about the details and the business end, but there is no substitute for being the person who has to make it all happen.

When I worked for myself, I didn't have the necessary mentality—I didn't have the courage to exist without the security blanket of a regular paycheck, and I didn't have the financial or emotional resources to ever feel at ease with that discomfort. My life had not yet prepared me with the confidence that I could do it on my own, and my faith wasn't strong enough to trust that everything would work out. I gave the solo thing a try for a year while having the crutch of a part-time job with another law firm. In the end, I don't think it was a mistake for me to open my own office nor to close it when it didn't feel right for me. Deep down, my real desire was to write—so ultimately all the different paths I've taken as a journalist and as an attorney ended up being steps on this journey, having their own sets of joys and regrets.

One of my closest friends grew up in Detroit and is the son of a business owner. He grew up seeing nothing but blacks owning their own businesses and succeeding. It was second nature for him to soar with an entrepreneurial spirit. Just like I had no experience seeing blacks work for themselves and do it successfully, he struggled with the concept that blacks should try to do it any other way.

Another alternative to working in primarily white workplaces or working for yourself is to seek out black-owned companies to work for. If you want to work for a big or medium-sized company, obviously those options are easier to find in larger cities with large black populations, such as Detroit, Atlanta, and Dallas. However, people are people, and the 85 percent issues matter just as much in black companies. It's about finding the right job, the right career, and the employer that matches what you need. Yes, you might not have to deal with a boss who doesn't "get" you because you're black, but a different kind of cultural bias can kick in. After all, a black executive who spent his summers on Martha's Vineyard may still have a huge disconnect from a brother or sister who spent his or her summers on the sidewalk with hip-hop and Kool-Aid.

The best option for your peace of mind may be to find another way to make a living, other than being a black employee at a white company. Because I was a lawyer, it's no surprise that a good deal of my friends are lawyers too. But as well as my lawyer friends and my old journalism friends, my circle of friends includes folks who work full-time as astrologers, feng shui consultants, massage therapists, and yoga instructors. Unlike half my friends who are lawyers and would rather be doing anything else, none of my friends with nontraditional jobs would rather be doing anything else. Now that's telling.

The most unhappy people I know are the folks who are frustrated because they would rather be doing something else—making music, teaching, filmmaking, or writing—but they find it easier to work for companies that provide regular paychecks. One of my favorite books is *The Artist's Way* by Julia Cameron. She writes about how many people are frustrated artists trying to quash their artistic spirits because society tells us that we need to have safe, reliable, grown-up jobs. I think this is particularly true of blacks who grew up with parents who had limited opportunities to have good jobs.

Everyone who has a dream has to decide if it's worth it to pursue the dream or let it ride. If you've got a spouse who depends on your regular income and children who expect to be fed, then being a "runaway slave" may not be a viable option. But part of keeping your life in balance is, hopefully, evolving in a way that allows you to make the difficult choices and find a place for your dreams!

Dozens of people have said to me, when they find out I'm a lawyer, "I've always thought about going to law school." My usual response is, "That's interesting, but have you ever thought about being a lawyer?" People usually get puzzled looks on their faces, because they haven't thought what they might want to do past law school graduation. They get caught up in the romantic vision of doing something other than what they are doing, without giving real thought to what they want to do the day after graduation. It's an example of the importance of moving toward something good instead of just away from something bad.

As black people, unfortunately, we have a greater tendency to limit our range of options because, historically, this country has done such a dandy job of limiting options for us first. There is a tale about an elephant trainer who tied one end of a rope around the leg of a baby elephant and the other end of the rope around the base of a tree. The purpose was to keep the baby elephant from wandering away, and the elephant could only walk as far as the rope tied to the tree allowed. Eventually the elephant trainer took off the rope, and the elephant spent the rest of its life never going farther than the length of that rope.

In so many ways, as blacks, we are like that baby elephant. The length of that rope (sort of like a noose) tells us we can be sports heroes and music stars, along with a few safe careers that already include a significant number of blacks, but we still struggle collectively when venturing beyond the confines of that rope. One of the reasons why it is so important to keep mental, emotional, physical, and spiritual balance in your life as a black employee is so you can know when you are feeling reined in. It's also important to keep that balance so you can know and feel when you are soaring to exactly where you want to be.

CONCLUSION

■

I LOVE BEING BLACK. I do. I love my people, our style, our culture, and our flavor in the melting pot.

But being black is a full-time job in America, and it's not a job that pays, so each of us must work it out along the way on our own time. As I said in the introduction, this world has changed beyond our wildest expectations. A man today can seriously think about staying home with his children in lieu of pursuing a career while his wife leaves the house every day to go to work. Although that still isn't common, fifty years ago it was science fiction. Fifty years ago, a black person would not have thought about sitting at the front of a public bus. Now a black person can drive a luxury car past a white person sitting at the bus stop. Again, it's maybe not the norm, but it's no longer extraordinary.

Success is the birthright of a black worker entering the workforce today, but discrimination, bigotry, and insensitivity still have place settings at the table. In seeing discrimination where none exists, we become our own worst enemy. In ignoring discrimination where it does exist, we are victimized without ever knowing there's been a crime.

My favorite definition of the word *magic* is what happens when intention meets attention. I believe that black employees can create magic in our working lives by knowing what we intend to achieve and paying attention to how we're getting there. Happy survivors may never pick up this book, because they don't need to know anything more than what the job requires. A desperate survivor may pick up this book wanting to know how to quickly make his or her working world all right again. Strivers—whether content or afraid—might pick up the book because they want any edge that gets them to what they are trying to achieve. Thrivers—whether cruising or fed up—may look at this book as a way to figure out how not to get trampled in the rat race.

But as any black employee who has gotten far enough in her life and career to have picked up this book in the first place should know, we're all in it together, and we all have the potential to be drivers. One black person's success is every black person's success. One black person's discrimination is every black person's sorrow. We're role models for each other—regardless of how much money or prestige our job has compared to someone else's. With our hair, clothes, speech, and attitude, we make the workplace browner, and the workplace is better for it.

Ultimately, you own your own experience as a black employee. You have to think, plan, prepare, observe, investigate, savor, and orchestrate every aspect of your job and career—and then, when necessary, you've got to do it all over again. Whether you're a street sweeper or a CEO, your job should reflect the glory of all the good choices you've made and all the adversities you've weathered along the way. The 15 percent issues will always arise, but you can achieve good results that are 100 percent yours.

Remember the rules of the road to arrive at a successful working life:

- How you start is how you finish.
- The proof is in the pudding, not the pudding mix.
- No matter what comes your way, you can create career magic when you combine intention with attention.

Good luck!

RESOURCES

■

Books

For Employment and Job Hunting

Bolles, Richard N. *What Color Is Your Parachute? A Practical Manual for Job-Hunters and Career-Changers.* Berkeley, CA: Ten Speed Press, updated yearly.

■ This widely used guide for job hunters and people changing careers has been updated and republished every year since 1976. It is particularly useful for those already in the workforce.

Covey, Stephen R. *The 7 Habits of Highly Effective People.* New York: Free Press, 2004.

- This classic book gives tools to improve personal effectiveness and leadership.

Deluca, Matthew J., and Nanette F. DeLuca. *More Best Answers to the 201 Most Frequently Asked Interview Questions.* New York: McGraw-Hill, 2001.
- This book gives you an idea of what employers commonly ask and what they are looking for so that you can prepare for a job interview.

Gladwell, Malcolm. *Blink: The Power of Thinking Without Thinking.* New York: Little, Brown, 2005.
- Gladwell explores the variety of ways people make decisions and choices, often unconscious and subconscious, which can explain how people view others of a different race.

Gladwell, Malcolm. *Outliers: The Story of Success.* New York: Little, Brown, 2008.
- Gladwell's second book identifies how success is not accidental but often a matter of timing, placement, and just putting in the hours it takes to succeed at something specific.

Johnson, Michelle T. *Black Out: The Black Person's Guide to Redefining a Career Path Outside of Corporate America.* Phoenix, AZ: Amber Books, 2006.
- I wrote this to give support and advice on how to create a life outside of traditional Corporate America, with options ranging from starting your own business to pursing art to working as an independent contractor to doing something totally out of the box.

Johnson, Spencer, M.D. *Who Moved My Cheese? An A-Mazing Way to Deal with Change in Your Work and in Your Life.* New York: G. P. Putnam's Sons, 2002.

- This is a little book about the big idea of figuring out your role in the dynamic of people trying to get ahead.

Jones, Charisse, and Kumea Shorter-Gooden. *Shifting: The Double Lives of Black Women in America.* New York: HarperCollins Publishers, 2003.
- These women explore the ways that black women have to "shift" to circumvent the dual biases of racism and sexism in our society.

Sinetar, Marsha. *Do What You Love, the Money Will Follow: Discovering Your Right Livelihood.* New York: Dell, 1987.
- This book gives step-by-step advice in finding the best work for you according to your needs and talents.

Other Helpful Books

Adrienne, Carol. *The Purpose of Your Life: Finding Your Place in the World Using Synchronicity, Intuition, and Uncommon Sense.* New York: Eagle Brook, 1998.
- This book emphasizes the importance of thinking outside the box to find your life's path.

Cameron, Julia. *The Artist's Way: A Spiritual Path to Higher Creativity.* New York: Jeremy P. Tarcher/Putnam, 2002.
- This is a great book on how to free yourself from being a "blocked creative" and live life on your own artistic path.

Choquette, Sonia. *Your Heart's Desire: Instructions for Creating the Life You Really Want.* New York: Three Rivers Press, 1997.

- This book covers nine universal, spiritual principles for transforming your life.

Gandy, Debrena Jackson. *All the Joy You Can Stand: 101 Sacred Power Principles for Making Joy Real in Your Life.* New York: Three Rivers Press, 2000.
- This is a guide on how to practice joy and experience renewal in all aspects of your life.

Grabhorn, Lynn. *Excuse Me, Your Life Is Waiting: The Astonishing Power of Feelings.* Charlottesville, VA: Hampton Roads, 2000.
- This book covers the importance of "energy" and how your feelings about and awareness of it affect every aspect of your life.

Greene, Bob, and Oprah Winfrey. *Make the Connection: Ten Steps to a Better Body—and a Better Life.* New York: Century Books, 1996.
- This is a ten-step exercise program from Oprah Winfrey and her personal trainer, based on getting to the root of what creates a weight problem in the first place.

Oliver, Stephanie Stokes. *Seven Soulful Secrets for Finding Your Purpose and Minding Your Mission.* New York: Doubleday, 2001.
- This is a book directed at black women, with good advice for both men and women on how to design a life that lets you be the best you can be.

Vanzant, Iyanla. *Acts of Faith: Daily Meditations for People of Color.* New York: Fireside, 1993.

- This is a guidebook of daily reflections geared to blacks on issues that touch on caring for both the self and the community.

Walker, Marcellus A., and Kenneth B. Singleton. *Natural Health for African Americans: The Physicians' Guide.* New York: Warner Books, 1999.
- In this book, medical doctors and other experts give advice on mainstream approaches and natural therapies for good health.

Web Sites

For Job Hunting

www.blackcareerzone.com
- This Web site for black career seekers includes articles and news.

www.careerbuilder.com
- This job-hunting Web site has a search engine, advice, and articles.

www.careerjournal.com
- This is the careers Web site of the *Wall Street Journal*; it provides daily articles, a tool kit for job hunting, discussion boards, a diversity section, and salary and hiring information.

www.careermag.com
- On this site, you can find job tips, include a photo with your posted resume, and receive automatic matches of your resume and job postings.

www.indeed.com
- This is a very good job hunting site that allows for a customized yet wide search by zip code.

www.linkedin.com
- This virtual networking site is good for just sticking to business.

www.monster.com
- On this site, you can post your resume, maintain a job search list, get information about benefits, and receive free newsletters.

For Legal Information

www.eeoc.gov
- This federal government Web site includes instruction on filing EEOC charges, information about mediation, and an overview of laws.

www.eeolaw.com
- This site provides articles, resume postings, and job searches and also includes information regarding scholarships, grants, and fellowships.

www.findlaw.com
- This is a general guide for information on legal resources, including a search engine for finding attorneys.

Other Helpful Sites

www.blackcollegian.com

- Billed as a "career site for students and professionals of color," this site features articles, offers information on graduate schools and military opportunities, and allows job searching and the posting of resumes.

www.blackenterprise.com

- This is an online guide to wealth building, finance, career, and small business opportunities.

www.diversityinc.com

- For a great Web site for articles and diversity resources of interest to all blacks in the workplace, check out this site.

www.workplacediversity.com

- On this site, you can post your resume and search for a job, find diversity news (sorted by minority group membership), and locate diversity organizations and employers.

INDEX

affirmative action, xxvi, 15, 53–54,
    62, 163–64; and Super Nig mental-
    ity, 52–53
Americans with Disabilities Act
    (ADA), 183
AOL Black Voices, 109
Artisan path, 27
The Artist's Way (Cameron), 238–39
at-will employment, 57, 101, 187–88,
    207

Baldwin, James, 169
Bennett, Milton, 72–73, 77
blacks: adult diabetes, 233; as "articu-
    late," 71, 161; assimilation, 209;
    attitude problem, 153–57, 161–62,
    164, 166–69, 173–75, 177; attitude
    problem, and black women,
    156–57; authenticity, 151; as
    authority figure, 167–68; back-
    ground check, 57–58; being black,
    as full-time job, xiv, 228, 241;
    black empowerment, xxvii; black
    tax, xiv, xvii; code switching of,
78–80; collective guilt of, 17–18;
    communication style of, 71; as
    communal, 120–21; Corporate
    America, as standing out in, 13;
    credit issues, 56; dialect, 81; GLBT
    community, 135–37; good commu-
    nication, as critical, 66; grooming
    of, 94–97; health care disparities,
    232; history of, as unique, 24–25;
    intention, 223, 242; job hunting,
    61, 63; job references, 62; job test-
    ing, 60–61; lawful questioning of,
    55–56, 59–60; obesity, 233; other
    ethnic groups, reaction to, 164–65;
    prayer, 230; race, as perennial fac-
    tor, 23; resiliency of, 29; respect,
    importance of to, 173–74; resumes,
    whitening of, 49–52; "runaway
    slave" mentality, 237, 239; smok-
    ing, 232; social networking of, 109,
    112–14; and speaking white, 71; as
    spiritual, 226, 231; standardized
    tests, and cultural bias, 60; stereo-
    types, battling of, 13, 16, 42, 53, 59,

•